Dedicated to

Miss Ellen Casey

First Among So Many

Other Books By James P. Walsh

San José State University: An Interpretive History, 1950–2000

Legacy of a Native Son: James Duval Phelan and Villa Montalvo
with Timothy J. O'Keefe

The Irish in the West
with Timothy J. Sarbaugh

San Francisco's Hallinan: Toughest Lawyer in Town

The San Francisco Irish

The Irish: America's Political Class

Ethnic Militancy

One and the Same: The History of Continuing Education at San José State University 1857–2007

James P. Walsh

San José State
UNIVERSITY

San José, California
2006

San José State University
One Washington Square
San José, California 95192

Book design by Heidi Heath Garwood, SJSU, B. A., Graphic Design, 1977
Book production by Nancy Roberts, SJSU, B. A., Commercial Art, 1967

Printed in the United States of America

Walsh, James P., 1937 –
One and the Same: The History of Continuing Education at San José State University
1857-2007 / James P. Walsh.
p. cm.
Includes index.
ISBN 0-9741479-1-5
Library of Congress Control Number: 2006939058

Table of Contents

Acknowledgements

The impetus to write this book came as a logical sequel to its predecessor, *San José State University: An Interpretive History, 1950–2000*. In composing that earlier volume I noted that the entire university enterprise and, therefore, the California State University System as well, originated as a continuing education enterprise. In that International and Extended Studies and San José State University share identical origins, both may correctly identify themselves as first among California's public institutions of higher education. They, and the California State University System, trace their history to Minns' Evening Normal School in San Francisco in 1857.

The leadership within International and Extended Studies, the modern extension office, recognized the historic position of Continuing Education at San José State University and asked me to develop its history more fully for the celebration of the university's sesquicentennial in 2007. This product is the result of the research and writing that took place through 2005 and concluded in 2006. Allow me to record my gratitude to an agreeable group of friends, colleagues and institutional staff members whose support and initiatives allowed the results to be as satisfactory as they may appear.

Dr. Mark Novak, Dean and Associate Vice President of International and Extended Studies, initiated the project and provided engaged encouragement and support throughout. Along with him Judy Rickard helped initiate the project and played a key role in converting my manuscript into the resulting product. Also, Dondi Bogusky served as the technology expert for the project and Farrukh A. Farid provided the initial hardware used in the research phase. Waynette Santos, John Fay and Sylvia Light provided editorial and proofreading expertise. Nadia P. Elliott coordinated all our meetings. Aparna Kanungo provided Open University enrollment data. Assisting with photography and providing photo consultation were Robert C. Bain, Reed Estabrook and Daniel P. Walsh. Photographic research, acquisitions and reproduction were facilitated by Elizabeth Burke Merriman, Thomas Carey, Robert Johnson, James R. Reed and Danelle Moon. Online searches, likewise, have become remarkable. Special thanks to Harriet Rochlin for facilitating acquisition of Hannah Marks' photo and to Elizabeth Burke Merriman for providing the photo of the Kennedy family.

Danelle Moon's role was expansive. Director of San José State University's Special Collections at the Dr. Martin Luther King, Jr. Library, she facilitated and encouraged my research. Her staff members took personal interest in the project and brought to my attention materials that I otherwise would have overlooked. They are Kaye Moore, Erin Louthen, Karla Aleman, Bernard Yeh and Russell Rader. For similar assistance and additional encouragement I wish to thank Jean Beard and Annette Nellen, colleagues in the search of our university's history.

Particular gratitude is due to the Office of the Provost and that of Faculty Affairs. Maria del Carmen Sigler and Joan M. Merdinger believed in this project. They advanced measurably San José State University's commitment to research by expanding the boundaries of scholarly access. Angee Ortega McGhee facilitated the documentary research. Carey Netzloff assisted with the ISBN process. The staff of the University of California, Berkeley's Bancroft Library, likewise, performed their historic services in support of research. Now, however, they do it promptly over the Internet.

Many persons who participated in the history of San José State University provided their recollections during taped interviews. I hereby acknowledge my gratitude. Many of their insights helped shape the interpretation that follows, whether their words are included or not. I wish to thank the following: Betty Benson, Ralph Bohn, Paul Bradley, Sharon Cancilla, Robert Donovan, Judith Kaiser, Khim Lok, Mark Novak, Karen O'Neill and Judy Rickard.

Lastly, my involvement in historical research and writing has changed greatly over the last five decades. Among other things, the process has become easier and ever more enjoyable. Perhaps retirement helps. What has remained unchanged is the warm support and practical help of my spouse, Ann McKinnon Walsh.

James P. Walsh

Los Gatos, California
January 15, 2006

Foreword

In this text, *One and the Same: The History of Continuing Education at San José State University, 1857–2007*, Dr. James P. Walsh presents a 150-year history of Continuing Education at San José State University – SJSU. He shows that Continuing Education (later International and Extended Studies – IES) and SJSU share a common origin. Continuing Education throughout its history dedicated itself to the service of the community, to the practical improvement of life, to personal growth of individuals, to innovation in the delivery and design of academic programs and to the recognition of international experience as a part of higher education. These same motives drive San José State University and International and Extended Studies today.

My own perspective on Continuing Education at SJSU takes up only a decade, or little more than six percent of Continuing Education's history at SJSU. This humbles me and puts my meager accomplishments in the context of an ongoing story. Dr. Walsh's work shows that many exceptional people shaped Continuing Education at SJSU throughout the years. In many cases the campus president took up the outreach mission personally. These presidents often used Continuing Education programs to advance the development of higher education at SJSU. In this way Continuing Education served as the source of innovation and educational progress.

Presidents and others took risks through Continuing Education programs that they could not take with the regular academic program. The invention of Open University, for example, opened the door to higher education for anyone interested in a university course. Continuing Education could introduce rapid and experimental changes in the curriculum. Non-degree credit courses, for example, could change each term according to the needs of the community.

Continuing Education could promote change that might be impossible if attempted through the core academic programs. Summer Session comes to mind as a key historic innovation. It served a social need, served the needs of individual teachers and generated income that served the whole campus. These multiple roles of Summer Session continued up to the start of this century. Newer programs like eCampus serve the needs of students and teachers who want access to education anytime, anyplace. More than 11,000 of San José State University's 30,000 students now take part or all of a particular course online.

eCampus marks the start of a technological revolution in education. But it stands in a long line of innovations pioneered by Continuing Education. Dr. Walsh's history shows that as student needs evolved, San José State University often met those needs through Continuing Education programs.

It has been a pleasure to consult with Dr. Walsh as he worked on this history. His dedication and skill as a historian surpassed my expectations. His work awakened in me a keen sense of the tradition of Continuing Education at San José State University. And it showed that the values of Continuing Education today— access, international programs and innovation—are woven through the history of SJSU. The service of Continuing Education to San José State University and the community has stood the test of time. This history tells the story of the first 150 years of Continuing Education at SJSU. It also serves as the starting point and guide for the future.

Mark Novak

Dean and Associate Vice President
International and Extended Studies
San José State University
San José, California
2006

Editor's Note

Throughout this book, continuing education as a concept or topic appears in lower case letters, regardless of the contemporary title of the division. Continuing Education as an office appears with capitalized words to show the distinction, regardless of the contemporary title of the division. The university name, with many changes through the years, is standardized as San José State University, the name of the university at the time this book was published. References to the original institution, Minns' Evening Normal School, appear, as well as occasional references to State Normal School, the early day San José campus and Normal Hall, the site of lectures and programs.

For a complete overview of the history of San José State University's names, see page 107. For a history of San José State University, see the companion volume, *San José State University: An Interpretive History, 1950–2000*, written by Dr. James P. Walsh, available at Spartan Bookstore on campus in the Student Union Building, 211 South Ninth Street, San José, California, 95112, 408-924-1800, 1-800-370-9794 or online at www.spartanbookstore.com.

Judy Rickard

SJSU, B. A. Journalism, 1970;
SJSU, M. S. Mass Communications, 1976
Marketing
International and Extended Studies
San José State University
San José, California
2006

Chapter One

One and the Same

Continuing education brought San José State University into existence. From that function sprang both the modern campus and the California State University System. Continuing education was their prime cause. And through the intervening 150 years the need for continuing education remained a driving force within the maturing university and the adult system of California higher education. The continuing education function was the essence of the university's generative DNA. Dominant at the start of institutional life and recessive into adolescence, continuing education grew abundantly through the 20th century. By the onset of the 21st century a dramatic though insufficiently noticed new stage beckoned – grand mutation.

That the university's origins were the origins of public higher education within historic California is well known. Equally clear are the story's 150 years of institutional stages: the normal school, the state teachers college and the comprehensive, metropolitan university. Until the late 20th century the university's central function remained teacher education. As a result San José State University history has generally been written as teacher education history. The advantage of greater perspective accompanying the university's sesquicentennial celebration is an appropriate time to begin a thematic re-examination. Changing vantage points ought, logically, to impact the historical perspective.

Educating the "Instant City"

The early development of public higher education in California came not from slow evolutionary changes. Instead, it quickly emerged from the social and cultural turmoil that constituted the California Gold Rush. The educational side effect of what became a massive, permanent and ever-expanding relocation of world populations created totally unanticipated results. The story actually transcends San José. What began so modestly in San Francisco became the largest centralized system of higher education in the history of world civilization. Within such a broad perspective the role of continuing education informs understanding of San José State University, the linchpin within California's educational accomplishment.

"Instant City" is the term historians use to capture San Francisco's invention of itself. The world that rushed in was largely male. Those early settlers looked upon their occupation of their environment as a temporary inconvenience. Why build houses, not to mention institutions, when all you wanted was to strike it rich and return home? And home could as easily be Connecticut, Chicago, Cork or Canton.

The original California dream, find gold and return home to a lifetime of improved circumstances, became a reality for the few. The many were divided between those who returned with more experiences than cash and those who simply remained. The new Californians then transformed their instant city from temporary base camp to the gold fields into the business, financial and cultural capital of the Far West. Educational institutions evolved as well. Again, need was the mother of invention.

During San Francisco's transformation the number of unschooled children became significant. Tutors and private schools, mostly under religious auspices, did not adequately meet the demand among elementary age children. This educational void existed at the same time as the New England states and New York vigorously advanced free public schooling.

In response to San Francisco's needs, enlightened leadership of an embryonic free public school movement stepped forward. The road, however, was never easy, particularly at the start. With no infrastructure existing in California, educational pioneers John C. Swett, Henry B. Janes and Andrew J. Moulder created a school system by accommodating local realities to the existing New England model. En route they initiated tax support, compulsory attendance, physical construction, curriculum design, staffing and academic standards. Their innovative response to the need for a competent teaching force is what ultimately created San José State University. The chosen method was continuing education. Their chosen delivery agent was George W. Minns and his Evening Normal School.

George W. Minns

Who Will Teach the Teachers?

The credentialing process of modern California public school teachers has grown to become a bewildering experience, particularly for seasoned teachers relocating to California and for Californians who decided upon teaching careers after first declaring an undergraduate major. In the 1850s California had yet to discover such credentials. School boards merely advertised in the newspapers for staff and interviewed the self-proclaimed teachers who presented themselves.

California history recognizes Minns for his founding role in the improvement and institutionalization of teacher education. He held leadership positions within the initial models, for both continuing education and the normal school.

George Minns had, himself, entered the educational field in California by responding to a San Francisco School Board advertisement. The recruits ranged in capacity from Minns, with bachelor and law degrees from Harvard College and an abiding interest in natural science, to teenage girls whose educational experience was that they had attended school. Not uncommonly, many applicants for teaching positions were still students themselves. At least one applicant whom the school board launched upon a highly successfully career may never have attended any school anywhere beyond her in-service hours at Minns Evening Normal. Such was the status of teacher qualification and such was the need for continuing education.

On such a teaching force parents and educators placed high expectations. They wanted enhanced knowledge, training, health and morality for San Francisco's growing number of children. Shortly thereafter local and state political leaders accepted the need for improved education as a means for establishing civic stability and advancing commercial enterprise. The impetus for education came not from within, but from outside the discipline. The teachers, clearly, lacked sufficient competence at their assigned tasks and disgruntled parents and more focused local educators became the instruments of change.

Minns, Swett, Moulder and Janes, like the founders of most enduring institutions, possessed the right mix. In their case zeal and competence were the givens. Innovation and salesmanship allowed the extraordinary success. All were dedicated advocates of free public schooling for California's children. Commanding various subjects and understanding the need for basic subject matter competency, they understood the place of educational philosophy and teaching methodology as the guiding constraints for the enterprise they were creating. Their marketing skills were clear, too. They established the stock and trade posture to be used by school board members and school administrators as advocates to the community of educational clients.

Defective Teaching

The first concern of San Francisco parents, at least among those who thought of the matter, was to get their children enrolled. In the 1850s some succeeded and some did not. Those who avoided enrolling their children actually had probable cause. Parents and newspaper readers alike learned of school and teacher limitations. Unskilled and unfeeling teachers brutalized students.

In the publicly celebrated case of 1853, for example, the court fined a teacher for whipping a disrespectful student "too severely." This was at a time in history when the consensus of both the masses and the learned approved of corporal punishment. The leading paper of the day, the *Alta California*, quoted the judge's observation that too many teachers "...had no control over their passions, and that too much beating blunted the sensibility of children instead of purifying their morals...." [1]

Further, the presiding judge returned the matter to the school board so that the constituted body would address its own problems. Pedagogy aside, the schools needed reforms if only to keep their deficiencies out of the courts and, thus, away from public view. Reform in the sense of comprehensive re-education was mandatory. The almost randomly acquired teaching corps of San Francisco's embryonic public schools needed professionalization. Beatings merely obscured the greater problem of competence.

The 1854 annual report that the office of the Superintendent of Public Schools submitted to the school board buried its assessment of teaching and simply admitted that, "It would be superfluous to say that the teaching has necessarily been somewhat defective...." Four years later Superintendent Henry B. Janes occupied stronger ground. He reported to a School Board President, Gold Rush merchant and importer William Sherman. He admitted to the teaching deficiencies that were already being addressed. Minns' Evening Normal School promised teacher remediation through the application of modern educational theory and the informed use of modern textbooks. [2]

Teachers who learned by doing needed a philosophical and methodological uplift. As well, they needed a plan to survive the next day's class and to advance their own career objectives. These are what Minns' Evening Normal School offered. The continuing education Monday night meetings addressed subject matter competency and the loftier principles of educational methodology and philosophy. By having required its already-employed teachers to enroll in Minns' Evening Normal School, a troubled school system committed itself to innovation and reform. In-service education was the means chosen to overcome classroom incompetence and to banish its accompanying brutality.

Despite teacher objections to the mandatory attendance policy, the school board remained resolute. Attendance continued as a condition of employment. Teachers either participated or risked being dismissed. The scheme had its own sweetener, however. Promotions within the teaching ranks followed from successful completion at Minns' Evening Normal School. From the beginning, then, what was a certificate program resulted in career advancement.

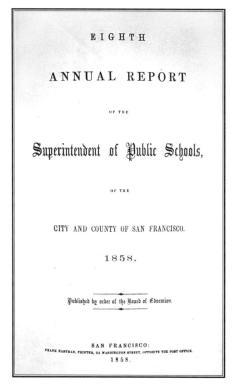

EIGHTH

ANNUAL REPORT

OF THE

Superintendent of Public Schools,

OF THE

CITY AND COUNTY OF SAN FRANCISCO.

1858.

Published by order of the Board of Education.

SAN FRANCISCO:
FRANK EASTMAN, PRINTER, 111 WASHINGTON STREET, OPPOSITE THE POST OFFICE.
1858.

Eighth Annual Report of the Superintendent of Public Schools, 1858, City and County of San Francisco, published by the Board of Education, 1858.

The First Classes

Professor Benjamin F. Gilbert's centennial history, *Pioneers for One Hundred Years: San José State College, 1857-1957*, chronicled the five-year history of Minns' continuing education efforts as prologue within the first century of San José State University's history. Twenty-first century research that anticipated the sesquicentennial of San José State University discovered additions to the story. The names of the day school teachers who were Minns' night school students came to light.

With 1857 as the accepted start, the Minns' Evening Normal School lived for five years. It graduated two classes, one in 1861 and the other in 1862. The first graduating class included 16 diploma recipients. All were women; one was listed as married. Each received her certificate because she earned a score of 70 percent or better on the comprehensive examination that covered the subjects contained in the continuing education curriculum. The same standard applied the following year when 38 students graduated. At this second and final commencement all graduates again were women, with seven listed as married. Though no special honors were mentioned, the premier graduate of Minns' Evening Normal School was Ellen Casey. She, therefore, is the first graduate of San José State University and the first graduate of the California State University System. Also, given the continuing education nature of Minns' Evening Normal School, Ellen Casey has the distinction of being the first graduate of a certificate program that was to create its own history in tandem with the state-supported normal, college and university. As such, Ellen Casey is the first graduate of the largest centralized institution of advanced education in the history of civilization.

Miss Ellen Casey

Miss Casey, as the era and her calling required her to be addressed, merits each of her historical distinctions because of her rank within the first graduating

ELEVENTH

ANNUAL REPORT

OF THE

Superintendent of Public Schools,

OF THE

CITY AND COUNTY OF SAN FRANCISCO,

1861-'62.

PUBLISHED BY ORDER OF THE BOARD OF EDUCATION.

SAN FRANCISCO:
MAGEE BROS. PRINTERS, NO. 230 MERCHANT STREET.
1863.

ABOVE: Eleventh Annual Report of the Superintendent of Public Schools, 1861-1862, City and County of San Francisco, published by the Board of Education, 1863.

RIGHT: Minns' Evening Normal School graduates, 1861 and 1862, published in above report.

GRADUATES OF 1861.

Miss Ellen Casey,	Miss M. A. Wills,
" M. A. Casebolt,	" C. L. Hunt,
" Alice Baker,	" D. S. Prescott,
" L. E. Field,	" M. L. Tracy,
" Eliza Hawkhurst,	" M. D. Lynde,
" Kate Kennedy,	" Hannah Marks,
" Lizzie Kennedy,	" Beatrice Weed,
" A. B. Kimball,	Mrs. A. E. DuBois.

GRADUATES OF 1862.

Miss A. S. Barnard,	Miss A. A. Rowe,
" C. V. Benjamin,	" E. R. Shaw,
" Anna Child,	" M. E. Stowell,
" C. A. Coffin,	" P. M. Stowell,
" L. H. Crocker,	" Helen Thompson,
" H. B. Cushing,	" E. M. Tiebout,
" E. P. Fernald,	" M. R. Warren,
" E. S. Griffin,	" M. C. White,
" H. A. Haneke,	" S. J. White,
" H. H. Heagan,	" L. A. Humphreys,
" Anna Hill,	" S. M. Hunt,
" M. A. Humphreys,	" Annie Lawrence,
" L. A. Humphreys,	Mrs. E. C. Burt,
" Lizzie Macy,	" E. S. Forrester,
" W. L. Morgan,	" L. A. Morgan,
" A. S. Moses,	" M. S. P. Nichols,
" H. E. Porter,	" H. E. Packer,
" Geraldine Price,	" C. H. Stout,
" M. E. Scotchler,	" S. A. D. Lansingh,

class. However, first in scholarship did not translate into first in career recognition and prominence in California history. Casey conceded those distinctions to Kate Kennedy, who ranked sixth among the initial 16 graduates. Immediately upon her completion of the certificate program, Kate Kennedy received promotion from classroom teacher to principal. For her this was one of the first important steps toward an abundant and well-recorded California career.

Four other students from Minns' first graduating class also merited historical attention. Mary A. Casebolt ranked second in the inaugural class. Lizzie Kennedy, Kate's sister, ranked seventh. Adelia B. Kimball ranked eighth and Hannah Marks ranked fourteenth. The merging of historic photography with digitization and the Web offer fresh and prompt insight into the circumstances of the women who accessed career advancement through continuing education.

Miss Mary A. Casebolt

Mary A. Casebolt's electronically reconstituted profile tells us a great deal about the initial graduates of Minns', San José State University and the California State University System. Her high school graduation photograph is on the next page.

Casebolt undoubtedly was still in her teens when she entered Minn's Evening Normal School and completed studies in 1861. She had graduated from the city's first high school in 1859. By these two distinctions Casebolt inaugurated a California elite, one of local educational attainment. Her co-founder of this new female elite was Adelia B. Kimball, who is shown seated next to Casebolt in the graduation photograph, second from the right. Casebolt and Kimball shared the distinction of being members of the first graduating class of the San Francisco high school and Minns' Evening Normal School.

Their high school photo reveals a class of 11 members, four of whom were young women. It offers no clue to rank within the class. Its archived existence and its fashionable content suggest a confidence and self-esteem of those being empowered by the education of the day. Complementary evidence implies the likelihood of vital interpersonal skills.

Mary Casebolt was one of 11 children. The Kennedy sisters populated a family of seven siblings. Both families had intense, but entirely different, American experiences. All understood how to negotiate with their peers as well as their

The first graduating class of the first high school in San Francisco, 1859. Mary A. Casebolt is seated, far right. Adelia B. Kimball is seated next to her.

siblings, not bad training for teaching. Historical assumption supports Miss Casebolt. Extensive documentation supports the Kennedy sisters.

Casebolt's genealogy extended back into American colonial and revolutionary history in which her forbears played contributory roles. In nineteenth century San Francisco her father, Henry Casebolt, gained fame and fortune as an inventor of novel cable cars and as owner of a successful rival to the city's hallmark system.[3]

The Casebolt family home, a three-story Italianate manor house in Pacific Heights, is Landmark 51 on the San Francisco Historic Landmark List.[4]

Casebolt seems not to have continued in teaching, at least in San Francisco, but the date of her marriage suggests that she may have had an intervening career. *The Overland Monthly* recorded her marriage to Horatio G. Finch in 1872.[5]

Misses Kate and Lizzie Kennedy

History reveals even more about the Kennedy sisters. Kate Kennedy's political, social and economic activism has attracted California historians. And her Irish family liked to write.

Unlike her youthful classmates at the evening normal school, Kate Kennedy was considerably older, 34 years of age upon graduation. Also, unlike Casebolt and Kimball, she was an immigrant. Her secure family of one brother, five sisters and mother fell upon hard times in Ireland with the early death of the father at age 41. That year, 1841, marked the curtailment of formal schooling for the Kennedy children in Ireland. Kate Kennedy was 14 at the time.

1857 Kennedy family portrait with Lizzie (standing, left) and Kate (seated, left), with their mother, Eliza King Kennedy, seated in center. Alice, standing second from the right, also taught school. The only brother, Patrick, became a San Francisco County Supervisor.

Alice Kennedy, who became a San Francisco teacher without graduating from Minns' Evening Normal School, was eight. And Lizzie Kennedy, who graduated seventh in Minns' class of 1861, was only three when their father died and the children ceased formal schooling. In terms of years of formalized education Kate Kennedy's record approached that achieved by Mary Casebolt. Alice Kennedy may have had two years at school in Ireland and Lizzie Kennedy would most likely have had none. Kate Kennedy home schooled all of her five sisters in Ireland, the most notable outcome being their commitments to lifelong learning and their facility with foreign languages. The siblings kept their diaries in French. Kate Kennedy, during her European sabbatical and other trips, conversed with continental educators and women's rights advocates in their own languages—French, Spanish and German.

From a woman's history perspective the three teacher-sisters exercised as many career options. Alice Kennedy relinquished teaching at the time of her marriage and become co-proprietor with her husband on their expansive sheep ranch and family estate that they created near San Luis Obispo.

Lizzie Kennedy embraced elementary teaching, marriage and family. She retired from the San Francisco public schools in 1914 at 80. Yet unfulfilled, she taught for another seven years in her daughter's private school, Miss Burke's School for Girls.

Kate Kennedy's career was a solo virtuoso performance through the fields of education, journalism, unionization, women's rights, national economic reform, philanthropy and freethinking. One specific and often-noted accomplishment was the temporary establishment in California of women's rights to equal pay for equal work. She accomplished this for her sisters in teaching through legislative action in 1874.

Miss Hannah Marks

Casebolt and the Kennedy sisters enjoyed family support. Hannah Marks arrived alone in California, chose not to marry her suitor-sponsor and turned to a career in teaching. Her marriage to community leader Gershom Mendes Seixas Solomons appeared successful to the public but was dysfunctional. Solomons' heavy drinking left her to raise their gifted and highly successfully children. While

Lizzy Kennedy's daughter founded an enduring private school, Hannah Marks Solomons' five children branched out. They mapped Yosemite, taught psychology, practiced law, practiced medicine and (like Kate Kennedy) wrote and advanced women's rights.[6]

Graduating within the first class of Minns' Evening Normal School was far from being the most important accomplishment in the eventful lives of these women. However, they grasped continuing education and used its opportunity to acquire security and fulfillment. Their jobs, their advancement and their career satisfactions emerged from continuing education. It was their enabler.

Hannah Marks

Chapter Two

Watching and Waiting

$\mathbf{M}$inns' Evening Normal School marked the start of what was to become an enduring and expanding educational enterprise. Minns' itself was merely transitional. In 1862, five years after its founding, the state legislature absorbed the evening normal school into California's initial effort for public higher education. Nine years later, in 1871, the legislature relocated the State Normal School from San Francisco to San José. By this move, Santa Clara County became the permanent home to the state's two historic universities, one private and the other public. Santa Clara University settled first into the county in 1851. Both initially focused upon their internal development and allowed leadership in continuing education to develop elsewhere among their university neighbors.

The younger and more precocious University of California (1868) and Leland Stanford, Jr. University (1885) temporarily filled the extension vacuum. Later, once its transition to State Normal School became secure, San José State University re-entered the field of continuing education. In the meantime, through to the end of

First San José Normal School building, destroyed by fire February 10, 1880.

Second San José Normal School building, c. 1900.

the 19th century, the State Normal School had much to observe, much to learn. En route the normal school gradually shifted from observer, to participant, to provider of continuing education.

For their parts the University of California and Stanford University had not yet approached great-university status. Both were in their early developmental stages. Both had a hard time attracting well-qualified faculty. They were properly positioned, though and enjoyed dynamic leadership of presidents who were to become institution builders. Benjamin Ide Wheeler directed Berkeley's advance for the Regents of the University of California. David Starr Jordan, under the watchful eyes of resident matriarch Jane Lathrop Stanford, did the same for Stanford. Each campus president understood continuing education and each president used extension in different ways to address community and university needs. With the State Normal School temporarily absorbed in its own institutional consolidation, both newer universities advanced their individual brands of extension into Santa Clara County.

Early Efforts by University of California

California's early take-charge man was Professor Charles Mills Gayley. Energized and competent, he virtually assumed the role of extended education provider for Northern California. As early as 1891 he enthused over the prospects of adapting the British model of university extension to the California opportunities he saw surrounding him.

Gayley's perspective, however, was from the university looking out upon a servile community, not the model that San José State University was to adopt once it re-entered the continuing education field. Gayley resided in a new university that lacked a sufficient number of students capable of meeting the entrance requirements. So challenged, Gayley's strategy was to upgrade and qualify more potential freshmen through outreach classes. A dynamic and successful university lecturer himself, he assumed that high-standard lecture courses would do the trick. The literature professor took pride in maintaining the same campus course standards for the continuing education courses. In fact, of the 1,230 extension students who sought university course credit, only 52 passed the screening examinations.[7]

Upon this philosophical basis, extension hardly prospered in California. So poorly begun, the early program failed to prosper under an even more dynamic and accomplished advocate, Professor Henry Morse Stephens. How Wheeler recruited Stephens also allows an insight into the financially manipulative side of continuing education as early as 1902.

To attract the highly regarded Stephens to California from Cornell, friend and former colleague Wheeler creatively met Stephens' salary demands. Wheeler gave him a dual appointment, professor of history and director of extended education. In practice the incomes and the obligations became oddly mixed. The director's salary was merely a top-off, but Stephens spent much of his time and energy with extended education. On the side the high energy, high capacity scholar published prodigiously and even wrote plays, one for the high jinks at the Bohemian Club's summer encampment in 1909.

The work-loving, travel-loving, cigar-loving Stephens offered university extension courses in what would later become the San José State University service area. He led the lecturing team and particularly loved meeting community organizers who served as local hosts for the extension lectures. Despite his networking and his personal charm, Stephens failed to create a successful, ongoing extension program. In the end, Wheeler sent his star performer south on an impossible mission.

Southern California had a large and growing population, one that needed more public higher education than the state was providing by a branch of the State Normal School. The populace and their state representatives demanded a branch of the University of California, too. Wheeler opposed the idea out of fear that the state would divide the University of California's resources with a non-Berkeley campus. So he resorted to a palliative. He attempted to satisfy the university needs of Southern California with extension lectures. Stephens died suddenly at the conclusion of World War I, just when University of California Los Angeles advanced to university status over Berkeley's opposition.

The University of California's brand of extended education failed to serve as a useful model for San José's State Normal School. The University of California's first attempt at extension education failed even in its own objectives. First, extension did not qualify students for Berkeley admission. Second, it did not restrict the university system to Berkeley. What it clearly illustrated was the institutional limits of popular lectures organized through multiple community groups. University extension lacked a specific clientele that was large, permanent, motivated and capable. Using extension for political objectives was improper and futile.

Stanford University Gets Involved

Stanford, though not public, was close, neighborly and interactive. The university's professors regularly traveled to San José to teach Monday, Wednesday and Friday night classes. San José's State Normal School reciprocated by providing the on-campus facility, Normal Hall, where the extension classes took place. What was remarkable about Stanford's extension was its academic quality delivered to intelligent, but popular audiences. The scholar-lecturers were commanding figures in their fields as well as public notables. Students and alumni of the normal school, seeking enhanced education opportunities, enrolled and participated.

A community organization, the University Extension Club of San José, facilitated the meetings of Stanford faculty at Normal Hall. A typical extension series included clusters of lectures under a general theme, all presented by a single extension instructor. Within this structure Stanford offered its academic stars and notables to the public.[8]

Stanford University president and distinguished scientist David Starr Jordan lectured in Normal Hall through the fall of 1892. His eight-lecture series included a popular presentation on how science explains natural phenomena such as the geysers of the American West. He also turned philosophical when he explained how science guides human understanding.

Jordan's large audiences included normal school students, schoolteachers, reporters and the interested public. The press offered extensive coverage for the readers of the *San Jose Daily Mercury*. Obviously cognizant of the perpetual

State Normal School faculty, students and visitors in Normal Hall, c. 1891.

controversy of evolution versus creation, Jordan clearly identified and isolated what constituted the domain of science. As if speaking to a modern-day audience, he explained the subject matter of science and the scientific method. With prudence, perhaps born of a university president as well as a scientist, he stopped at the border of religion. He did so in such a way that his evening listeners and the

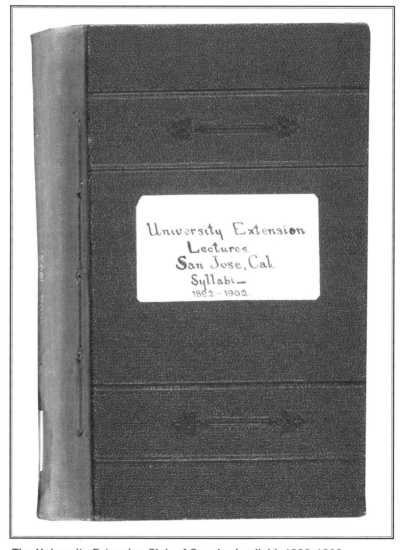

The University Extension Club of San José syllabi, 1892-1902.

~~~THE~~~

UNIVERSITY EXTENSION

~~~CLUB~~~

OF SAN JOSE.

SEASON OF 1893=94.

The Present Battle-grounds of Evolution

DAVID STARR JORDAN,

David Starr Jordan's University Extension Club of San José syllabus.

morning readers knew what was nonscientific. Decades later, in the 1920s, Jordan testified as a defense witness in the famous Scopes trial where he explained the scientific validity of the theory of evolution.

Neither Jordan's celebrity as a university president nor his reputation as a scientist created any aloofness. In order to accommodate his State Normal School students before their Christmas vacation in 1892, he adjusted his lecture schedule to accommodate their holiday break. To do so, he twice more traveled from Palo Alto to the normal school campus, once on a Saturday and again on the following Monday evening. He inconvenienced himself so that the students might receive their full measure of the extension course in which they had enrolled.

President Jordan's most notable Stanford colleague to serve in a continuing education capacity on the normal school campus was Professor Edward A. Ross, who followed Jordan during the next year, offering a cluster of lectures under the theme of "Modern Industrial Unrest." Timely and provocative, the committed Stanford sociologist displayed a command of his subject equal to that of Jordan's, but fell short of his president's discretion. Ross's conclusion, proclaimed at San José's State Normal Hall and covered in the *San Jose Daily Mercury*, was that across America "the general tendency now is toward socialism, separate from the state and law." So, according to the Stanford scholar, socialism was on the march despite the U.S. Congress and the judicial system of the nation.

Consequences of Unpopular Views

Normal Hall was one of numerous venues where Ross restated his professional conclusions. Ross's statements and the press they attracted quickly exceeded the forbearance of Jane Lathrop Stanford — the university's surviving founder, patron and employer of both Ross and Jordan. Acquiescing to Mrs. Stanford's enduring authority, Jordan dismissed Ross from the Stanford faculty in 1900. The result was a national cause celebre in the history of academic freedom and faculty tenure. During the uproar at Stanford another faculty member, Professor George Elliott Howard, was terminated for the vigor of his protests in support of Ross. Other faculty resigned, protesting both dismissals.

Howard and Ross accepted major academic appointments at Nebraska and Wisconsin, and in turn both accepted honor from their professional colleagues and served as presidents of the American Sociological Society. Ross became an icon for academic freedom, all the more celebrated because of subsequent national acclaim given his cutting edge books and articles that energized American thought for the Progressive Movement.[9]

San José State Normal School students, faculty and administrators witnessed the richness of this academic ferment at very close range. Continuing education gathered the players. Continuing education students and those who read class content in the morning papers experienced not just the stuff of academic lectures. In this case scholarship's informing power had been exciting as well. Insightful local educators observed the opportunities for homegrown continuing education. If mass clientele could be substituted for controversy, perhaps the normal school might become a player of substance too.

Chapter Three

The Critical Choice

Basic change of functions accompanied the state legislative action that converted Minns' Evening Normal School into the California State Normal School. Legislation in 1862 allowed for the normal school's relocation from San Francisco to San José, a move that took place in 1871. The same legislation also induced a 41-year dormancy of the original continuing education function that Minns' had fulfilled. For its part the California State Normal School relinquished continuing education in 1862 only to re-enter the field in 1903.

The California State Normal School's mission was the training of new teachers for new careers in California's new and expanding schools. The state legislature effected this change by requiring the State Normal School to operate during the day, five days a week, for five months each year.[10]

The same legislation that authorized this major redirection away from in-service education also contained the reasons for the re-emergence of Continuing Education four decades later. Under the original legislation, students were admitted to the State Normal School at very early ages, 15 for females and 18 for males. By accommodating the educational realities of the day, the legislature also created the future opportunity for San José State University to reenter the continuing education field. Young beginning teachers remained at their careers while the standards under which they qualified became outmoded.

By the 20th century, San José's State Normal School had welcomed the creation of four additional State Normal Schools: Chico, San Francisco, Los Angeles and San Diego. Through these decades San José State University maintained its own premier status as the first and the largest State Normal School. Persisting in its assigned function, the school added to its large, expanding and alert constituency— California's schoolteachers. Broader forces, of course, played their part as well.

Population growth, California's permanent phenomenon, was the first social force to be negotiated. The ideology that accompanied this demographic change sustained public policy favoring free public education. The state, as the guardian of a democratic society, required ever-improving education that guided and informed the citizenry and energized the economy. These two forces, ever increasing population and ever rising standards for free public education, reawakened the continuing education function at San José State University. Besides minting more teachers, the normal school needed to upgrade its large alumni.

State Normal School class of 1878 with State Normal School building at bottom row, center.

The normal school's leadership, who bridged the transition into the 20th century, chose wisely among its options. Presidents James McNaughton and Morris E. Dailey recommended summer school as the initial solution to the problem of educational lag among schoolteachers.

President Morris Dailey planting a tree with Professor Henry Meade Bland (wearing skull cap).

Summer School Arrives

The terms of teacher employment required supplemental education. Schoolteachers had the time, the resources and even the enthusiasm to comply. Because they resided all over California, the night school model of Stanford and The University of California would not do. Their flexible time was in the summer. During that time they were more than willing to come to San José to advance their education at what, additionally, became a nice experience—one they could repeat. What was more, by the dawn of the 20th century, the normal school had become entirely capable of delivering this form of instruction. It was to become continuing education on the San José State Normal School model.

Planning for summer session preceded its creation, but not by much. James McNaughton's single year presidency, 1899–1900, began with a virulent local political attack against him. The alumni association leadership joined the protest, assailing McNaughton's character and his fitness to lead the normal school. Calm returned only after McNaughton and his attorney, J. R. Patton, personally defended his appointment before the Board of State Normal School Trustees, the presidential appointing body. The beset trustees deliberated, reaffirmed the correctness of their original appointment and then urged peace and cooperation among all those interested in the normal school's welfare.

Though poorly begun, the 1899–1900 school year advanced quite successfully under McNaughton's steady management. His gift for clear and orderly communication helped. Among his well-worded recommendations to the trustees was the first call for a summer session. In his report of March 22, 1900, he projected what was to become a staple for San José summers, for the normal school and for the city. He wrote:

> The time has come for this school to hold a summer session each year.... It would afford an opportunity for those already engaged in teaching and who are in need of normal training, to attend the Normal School during the vacation period.... The great outlay of this State in the equipment of Normal Schools ought to be made to yield the greatest possible educational return to the people.[11]

Rather than approve McNaughton's recommendation, one whose time had come, the trustees terminated him. Centennial historian Benjamin F. Gilbert considered this action to have been scapegoating. The trustees defended their own integrity in McNaughton's appointment, survived the year and then surrendered to his alumni opponents. Additionally, the trustees terminated seven faculty members, some with 20 years of service. Seven others resigned. Rather than tumult, harmony and ordered growth followed, including the re-emergence of continuing education.[12]

President Morris E. Dailey deserves the title of founder of San José State University's Summer School. This distinction was but one among the many that Dailey earned through his long and highly successful 1900–1919 presidency. Dailey embraced the wisdom of McNaughton's message to the trustees even though the trustees had executed the messenger. Daily went further and spelled out a revised annual school calendar for the trustees to consider, "...two terms of eighteen weeks each, and a summer school of six weeks, especially adapted for Teachers and more advanced students."[13]

President Dailey directed his lobbying efforts at two fronts. First, he informed the trustees that only eight percent of the state's public school teaching force held bachelor's degrees and only 29 percent held diplomas from normal schools. The problem was clear, and Dailey committed himself to the summer session as the solution.[14]

President Morris E. Dailey

Second, Dailey drew McNaughton's harshest critics to support his plan. After all, the school-teaching alumni should not become summer school critics. They should become its clientele. Prudently, Dailey created a summer planning committee and had it meet with a counterpart from the alumni association. Together they approved the plan. The business community, likewise, favored a summer influx of teachers from around the state. With his ducks in line, the savvy president moved ahead.[15]

Opening on June 29, 1903, San José State Normal School enrolled 107 students in its inaugural summer school—a full twelve-week program that concluded on September 18th. Ten days into the inaugural summer school, enrollments jumped from 107 to 153.[16]

Summer School Takes Off

These statistics immediately became the boilerplate that year after year, decade after decade, characterized the abundant press coverage of summer school. At the start of the century, however, all this was new and it was exciting. The newspapers, always receptive, treated San José State University for what it had become—the largest and most important institution in town. Even the summer curriculum was news. If you missed the first class, you were encouraged to show up anyway. Instructors offered make-up classes. Later, when telephones became common, numbers were included and you could even talk to the teachers at home. As long as San José remained agricultural and commercially underdeveloped, San José State University's local marketing needs remained easily and inexpensively satisfied.

As McNaughton and Dailey anticipated, summer attendees gathered from all over California, then from across America and even from abroad. Housing accommodations, retail shops, restaurants and recreation venues shared in the energizing side effects. Dailey and his successors always delivered a faculty, a curriculum and an enthusiasm that met the advancing career needs of their students. Their careful management of the internal dynamics generated success. Outside forces, though, were the determinants.

Well begun in 1903 and increasingly successful through 1905, the summer school suffered a major interruption with the earthquake and campus damage of April 1906. Following the rupture along the San Andreas Fault, many day classes met outdoors during the spring term. Confronted with the damage and dislocation, President Dailey canceled the summer school planned for 1906 but quickly reinstituted it for 1907 and 1908 only to have the campus-rebuilding program intervene once again during the summer of 1909. Dailey availed himself and San José State University of the break by initiating travel education in the summer of 1909. He resumed planning but the World War I years delayed the full revival of Summer School until 1918. Thus, natural disaster, reconstruction and war disrupted what had been an immediately accepted and successful program. Dailey's support of summer education prevailed over any residual threats from the Spanish Influenza pandemic.

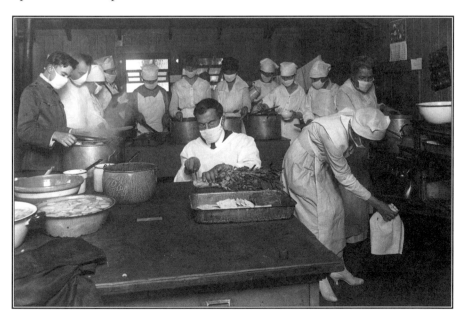

State Normal School volunteers preparing food during the influenza epidemic, 1918.

Institutional permanency arrived in 1922. In that year Summer Session became a fixed part of the academic calendar at San José State University. Summer School founder President Morris E. Dailey died unexpectedly in 1919. Yet the program he initiated in 1903 and reconstituted in 1918 bloomed during the century that followed. Summer School became the institution's customized response to the continuing education needs of its core clientele. Numbers and needs were the driving forces of growth as an ever-expanding California teaching force relentlessly pursued career development. Natural forces, the economy and world affairs were the broader, though only occasional, retardants. The state's 1921 reorganization of higher education actually solidified Summer School's success.

Campus Gets a New Name

Until that year the state board of trustees had overseen teacher education via the normal schools. The board, which came into existence with the conversion of Minns' Evening Normal School to California State Normal School, performed its final duty in 1921. Before surrendering authority to the California State Department of Education, the trustees recognized San José State University's development and renamed the normal school. On July 30, 1921, the normal school became San José State Teachers College. This heralded event masked the quiet advancement of Summer Session and Continuing Education as well.

The transition leadership appointed to San José State Teachers College by the outgoing board of state normal school trustees and then by the new department of education favored the continuing education function. The trustees' final presidential appointee was William W. Kemp in 1920. Kemp was a professor of educational administration from the University of California and an educator of international accomplishments. He took a two-year leave from Berkeley in order to bring San José State University from normal school to teachers college status. Deep within President Kemp's resumé was a three-year appointment as director of summer sessions at the University of Montana. While presiding over the transition to college status, Kemp institutionalized Summer Session at San José State University. As well, he inaugurated an extension service whose destinies were to become far-reaching.

New Acting President

Almost as a safeguard to Summer School's place at the teachers college, the new state department of education filled a potential leadership vacuum for the summer of 1923. The department installed its own financial expert, Alexander R. Heron, into the acting presidency for the summer only, a bridge between Kemp and President Edwin R. Snyder. Summer School thrived, as did all other responsibilities tended by Heron who, in fact, was a skilled professional administrator.

Heron's long career featured expanding responsibilities in and out of state government. After his Progressive Era service to California finance and education he became vice-president and director of the Crown Zellerbach Corporation. Then he directed World War II federal agencies managing the home front economy. And in post-war California he directed the state reconstruction and re-employment operations. His career role was that of an immensely capable, obscure bureaucrat who surfaced once and briefly at San José State Teachers College. While there he assured the place of Summer Session and made the path clear for the institution's future.

His summer enrollment marked a new high water mark, 620 students. More important, Heron contributed educational vision and financial planning expertise to the campus and to the evolving system of state colleges. His primary contribution was to establish clearly and publicly that California higher education was permanently changed. No longer was the old and surprisingly enduring apprentice system of teacher preparation acceptable. No longer should teachers learn in their positions. No longer was normal school training adequate. Teachers college completion was the new standard for California schoolteachers.

New School Staff Standards Proposed

If the new standards that Heron proclaimed for staffing public schools remained fixed and not again raised, and if the California student population remained stable, perhaps state teachers colleges could prepare the necessary number of new teachers. This once-and-for-all goal remained a mirage, though. Neither condition was to prevail and the distant goal was never attained. Always-improving standards and always-increasing populations maintained the always-enduring gap that continuing education addressed. Twentieth-century California schoolteachers continued to be a large and ever-growing clientele. They were educationally needy, but financially secure. They were politically savvy and possessed their own professional organizations that clarified and communicated their wishes. Those same organizational structures allowed San José State University easy and efficient contact with the membership. Reaching the far-flung schoolteachers of the vast state with news of continuing education offerings was hardly a marketing challenge.

Summer School Changes San José Community

As years passed and student numbers grew, the San José community adjusted to its role as host. At first, young women from outlying districts resided for the summer in the homes of their local relatives or friends. Room, then apartment,

Summer School 1936 schedule.

SAN JOSE STATE COLLEGE BULLETIN 9

COURSES OF INSTRUCTION—Continued

No.	Title	Hour	Room	Instructor
	NATURAL SCIENCE			
Nat. St. 15	Nature Study for Primary Grades	7	S207	JACOBS
Gen.Sci.120	Teaching of General Science	8	S112	BRAUER
Nat. St. 20	Nature Study for Intermediate Grades	8	S207	JACOBS
Agri. 1S	General Agriculture	9	S210	BOTTS
Photo. 10	Photography for Fun (Fee to be arranged)	9	S112	BRAUER
Biol. 25S	Native California Trees, Shrubs and Flowers	11	S207	JACOBS
Phys. 52S	Physics of Everyday Life	11	S210	BOTTS
Astr. 101S	Descriptive Astronomy	1	S112	BRAUER
Chem. 10S	Chemistry of Everyday Life	1	S210	BOTTS
	PHYSICAL EDUCATION (Men)			
199S	Problems in Physical Education	1	11	DEGROOT
2S	Swimming and Diving (MTWTh) (Fee 50c) (½ unit)	2	Pool	DEGROOT
18S	Tennis (MTWTh) (Fee 50c) (½ unit)	3	Courts	DEGROOT
10S	Recreational Games (MTWTh) (Fee 50c) (½ unit) (Badminton, teniquoits, ping-pong, horseshoes, volley-ball, softball, etc.)	4	Courts	DEGROOT
19S	Golf (Special rate of $6 for period of summer school, Saturday afternoons and Sundays excluded.) (½ unit)	Hours to be arranged	Hillview Golf Course	DEGROOT
	PHYSICAL EDUCATION (Women)			
18S	Dancing (Theory and Practice) (Fee 50c) (1 unit)	7	W.G.	LUCAS
16S	Primary Activities (Theory and Practice) (Fee 50c) (1 unit)	8	W.G.	KNAPP
23S	Teaching of Posture (Theory and Practice) (Fee 50c) (2 units)	8	W.G.	LUCAS
17S	Intermediate and Junior High Activities (Theory and Practice) (Fee 50c) (1 unit)	9	W.G.	KNAPP
106S	Organization of Physical Education (Lect.) (2 units)	10	W.G.	KNAPP
6S	Swimming (MWF) (Fee 50c) (½ unit)	4	Pool	LUCAS
8S	Badminton (MWF) (Fee 50c) (½ unit)	4	W.G.	KNAPP
21S	Social Dancing for Junior and Senior High Schools (Theory and Practice) (MW) (Fee 50c) (2 units)	7 to 9:30 p. m.	W.G.	LUCAS
	PSYCHOLOGY			
150	Educational Psychology	8	116	DEVOSS
114 or 214	Methods in Mental Diagnosis (Fee $1)	8	114	HEATH
116 or 216	Mental Hygiene	9	116	DEVOSS
101	Educational Measurements (Fee $1)	9	114	HEATH
150	Educational Psychology	11	116	DEVOSS
151 or 213	Adv. Educational Measurements (Personality Testing) (Fee $1)	11	114	HEATH
	SCHOOL OF THE THEATER (See also Speech)			
104A	Play Production	8	53	GILLIS
126	Design in the Theater (2 to 3 units)	9	53	GILLIS
55A	Acting (1 to 3 units)	9	55	CLANCY
116	Makeup (Fee $1) (1 to 3 units)	11	53	CLANCY
110A	History of the Theater	1	53	MENDENHALL
124A	Voice and Diction (2 to 3 units)	2	155	MENDENHALL
57A	Laboratory Theater (1 to 3 units)	3 to 5	53 and 55	STAFF
	SOCIAL SCIENCE			
Pol.Sci.150S	Current Political Issues	8	11	POYTRESS
Soc.Sci. 150	Problems of Social Security	9	11	POYTRESS
Soc.Sci. 190	Teaching of Social Science	11	11	POYTRESS
Hist. 179	Contemporary World History	11	30	WHEELER
Hist. 189	History of California	1	30	WHEELER
Pol.Sci. 75	American Constitution	2	30	WHEELER

An illustrative internal page of Summer School 1936 schedule.

rentals followed. After mid-century, San José State University's summer programs attracted out-of-state teachers who not only brought their families with them, they brought their house trailers, too. During the week they occupied local facilities. On weekends they drove into the Santa Cruz Mountains with Big Basin State Park being among the popular retreats.

The prize for student adaptability, however, belonged to the unnamed enrollee cited by Registrar Joe H. West in 1943. That student attended 12 consecutive summer schools beginning in 1932 and worked swing shifts at the local fruit canneries.[1/]

Until Dean Leo P. Kibby alerted his summer students of impending Internal Revenue tax revisions in 1966, the schoolteachers enjoyed a welcome bonus. They had become comfortable in deducting their summer fees, travel and living costs as business expenses. Those who moonlighted while attending Summer School earned income with full expensing.

The Summer School faculty constituted a flexible mix of resident instructors, augmented by local and state educational functionaries, artists and professors of national reputation. Leadership and finances determined the combination. Until the advent of a truly professionalized and tenured college faculty, teachers pretty much did as they were told—even at the college level. Through the early 20th century, college faculty also played educational catch-up by acquiring advanced degrees while employed, analogous to their own summer students. In advance of an absolute requirement that the college faculty possess terminal university degrees, top San José State University administrators came to possess these credentials. Early faculty members were subordinate, and they knew it.

For example, President Dailey's first Summer School teachers, recruited from his regular faculty, taught without any pay. He reported this fact to the trustees as a favorable condition. Records have not revealed if the president's genuine charm sufficed, or if his leverage in the situation made subtle intimidation unnecessary. Later, an honorarium of $25 sufficed.

Early administrative apparatus, likewise, was simple and free. No separate organization managed the first summer schools. The presidents and the few they drew into part-time administrative roles merely added the new responsibilities to their previous activities. They apparently received no added compensation. While he was Acting President (1925–1927) Herman F. Minssen doubled as the Summer School financial officer. President Thomas W. MacQuarrie participated in the weekly, if not daily, functioning of the summer school, even after the creation of an office which was assigned the management tasks. MacQuarrie's administrative oversight, however, had larger purpose. He, much like Dailey, understood what he was about.

During the Great Depression of the 1930s state regulations required President MacQuarrie to submit his faculty list for the upcoming year for review by successive state superintendents of public instruction. MacQuarrie fulfilled this requirement in person and, while doing so, invited his bureaucratic superiors to San José to visit the summer school. When they visited, he honored them as educators of distinction. Superintendent of Public Instruction Vierling H. Kersey closed Summer School in 1934 with his own four-part lecture series delivered in Morris Dailey Auditorium. His captive audience, besides the gracious President MacQuarrie, was the entire summer faculty and student body. On one evening of his four-day visit Kersey spoke to a more intimate gathering outdoors at the recreation amphitheater. On a second evening he accepted the honors of a Kappa Delta Pi banquet at Hotel de Anza. President MacQuarrie refined and re-ran his Summer School routine for educational dignitaries over the years.[18]

Summer School teaching and management became outlets for talent, energy and ambition. Many participants, from George E. Freeland in the first quarter of the 20th century to Ralph C. Bohn in the century's last quarter, advanced through Summer School to higher administrative posts. Two Summer School and Continuing Education administrators, Freeland and James C. DeVoss, were campus presidential candidates. A third, Raymond M. Mosher, accepted a presidential appointment at Eastern Washington College of Education. Their leading colleagues in extended education became administrators and deans. DeVoss enjoyed immediate prominence as a published scholar. Freeland traded teaching and administration in San José for a new career as a professional writer working from New York. Joe H. West, restricted because he lacked a doctorate, became San José State University's most accomplished professional administrator.

Summer School Changes SJSU

Summer School at first mirrored the curriculum of the year-round college. Later it augmented and enhanced it. The 175 schoolteachers who arrived on June 29, 1903 encountered the full, regular year course offerings. This policy, followed by the normal school, the teachers college and the university, allowed summer students to earn units, diplomas and degrees while maintaining their regular employment. Changes in the size and content of the curriculum reflected the growing sophistication of the university and new demands placed upon public schoolteachers.

Experimentation remained subordinate to dependability and relevance as Summer School courses approximated the standard year-round offerings. Basic change accompanied changes in state credentialing requirements. These changes took place after consultation with district, county and state school superintendents.

Even as late as the 1960s when the baby boom generation departed the public schools and teacher hiring ceased, the state colleges still reserved 20 percent of their summer curriculum for professional education. Of course, most of the remaining 80 percent addressed its new clientele, regular students advancing their degree programs. Innovation and the spirit of entrepreneurialism, likewise, were in evidence before the information technology revolution impacted Silicon Valley and San José State University.[19]

Celebrations, enrichments and the intrusions of broader American life spiced and leavened the Summer School century. Acting Dean of Educational Services and Summer School Dr. William G. Sweeney prepared the way for San José State University's "Golden Summer School" by sending 20,000 spring announcements to prospective attendees. Despite selecting the incorrect date, 1954 rather than 1953, the golden-plus-one Summer School offered an ambitious and expansive program. Financially sound and self-supporting, the program offered two sessions—one of six weeks and the other of four.

Ambitious spirits opting for both—ten weeks of classes—could accrue a quarter term's credits toward degree acquisition. The total schedule of classes listed more than 250 courses extending from aviation to travel education. In cooperation with the California Teachers Association, Summer Session highlighted an educational tour of Scandinavia that included two weeks residence each at the University of Oslo and educational institutes in Sweden and Denmark. Doris Linder of the education department, a Swedish speaker and former teacher of English in Sweden, led the summer school party.

Meanwhile, Summer School back home served a student body that exceeded 3,000 attendees. The faculty had grown to 172, a number that included 50 academic visitors. The distinguished guest faculty gathered to San José from Pennsylvania State, Boston, Stanford and Brigham Young Universities, University of Hawaii, the Rochester public schools, as well as from Sacramento—notable educator-bureaucrats from the state department of education. From the resident and imported talent, Sweeney's staff mounted journalism and teacher-training workshops, dramatic productions, natural science field studies, art exhibitions and celebratory concerts.[20]

Twice, Joe H. West stepped beyond his merged Summer School and Continuing Education role to organize major institutional celebrations. In 1957 he directed the centennial of San José State University's founding. In 1962 he did the same for the centennial of the institution's charter by the State of California. Summer School's 70th birthday organizers began by choosing the right anniversary year to celebrate — 1973. Paul M. Bradley, the associate dean, offered Summer School's customary spring press release and touted the real progress through seven decades. Enrollment for the anniversary year would nudge 10,000. Bradley intended to accommodate the new record high in three sessions: four, six and ten weeks. Special recreational events were included, but those were becoming standard by the early 1970s. Bradley stressed the basics and opened the classes to more potential students. He invited non-student adults and adolescents to explore their own educational options.

Bradley encouraged high school seniors and juniors to try out college and even get a head start toward a degree. They could acquire from three to six units of college credit from among a customized program of individualized projects in natural science and introductory courses in psychology, anthropology, philosophy and communications. For the summer student body at large Bradley offered much more, 800 courses, 30 of which were available in the evening. The public spokesman for Dean Ralph C. Bohn, Bradley used the 70th birthday celebration as a marketing point in publicizing a solid program.

Dr. Bohn had succeeded Dean Leo P. Kibby in 1970. He was experienced and highly energetic. So was his staff. Celebration '83, Summer Session's 80th birthday, reversed the protocol. Dean of Extended Education Ralph C. Bohn stepped into the public light, greeted the well wishers and commenced partying.

Dean Bohn presided over multiple celebrations, ice cream and coffee near mid-day and a full barbecue later in the afternoon. To create the birthday atmosphere appropriate to the first normal school summer session on the Pacific Coast, the staff came in historic attire. Young men in their flat boater hats minded by stern schoolmarms were much anticipated, but the keystone cop actually captured everyone's attention. After all, at parties law and order had to be preserved, too. Youthful Judy Rickard, who was to guide extension marketing into the 21st century, worked the crowd and infused the festivities with charm and goodwill.

Former Dean Kibby attended and offered his own congratulatory words. His predecessor, Dean West, retired for 18 years and residing beyond the Bay Area, could not attend. He conveyed his enduring goodwill to the university and the very special program he had nurtured into the modern world of extension. Bohn, the main speaker, offered Continuing Education's vision. In his view, extension would "continue to grow and adjust with the changing needs of the people of California." Aware of the growing impact of numerous technologies upon education, Bohn expected that technology would play a major role in the future of Continuing Education.

Less a visionary than a dynamic manager, Bohn looked to the system and his network of professional associations in which his career had matured. Bohn saw more clearly that the laws and regulations of the state and the policies of the chancellor's office had to be modified and liberalized for Continuing Education to assume its destiny.

Into the early evening, Kibby, Bohn, Bradley and the staff mingled among the campus celebrants. Missing, of course, were the numerous students who were enrolled in off-campus programs located elsewhere throughout Santa Clara County and Northern California, up in the Sierra Mountain Range and across Europe, Asia and Latin America. E-students in eCampus remained for the future, but they were gathering.

Summer School's offerings in the performing arts blossomed whether a special anniversary occurred or not. And the productions constituted the major cultural contribution to the community. Summer '65 offered its Summer Festival of Arts that included music recitals by solo performers, faculty concerts by the Summer Session Orchestra and Chorus, as well as popular street performers of the '60s— the San Francisco Mime Troupe.

The talented and already experienced Dr. Hal J. Todd joined the Drama Department the previous year and for Summer Festival '65 focused on the works of Irish playwrights. Over the Summer School weekends, students and townsfolk enjoyed George Bernard Shaw's works "Major Barbara" and "Shewing Up of Blanco Posnet," Sean O'Casey's "Shadow of a Gunman" and "Bedtime Story" and John Millington Synge's "Shadow of the Glen."[21]

For the summer of 1970, drama chairman Todd positioned theater more prominently within the Summer Festival of Arts. During the six-week Summer Session Todd directed Lillian Hellmann's drama "The Little Foxes" and George M. Cohan's spoof "The Tavern." Richard Parks, a lecturer in the Drama Department, directed "The Apple Tree" that included three musicals, playlets from Mark Twain, Frank R. Stockton and Jules Pfeiffer. The Drama Department, via Summer School, extended the performing arts link to the community. En route, San José State University and Summer School enjoyed extensive press coverage, lavish with photography. [22]

Meeting the Challenges

Summer School's historical mantra—bigger and better—faltered occasionally when outside forces intervened. The 1906 Earthquake and World War I witnessed program suspensions. In the case of the Great Depression and World War II, program innovation trumped crisis. The GI Bill and the arrival and departure of the baby boomers were more complicated phenomena and brought forth comparable responses.

By the 1930s Summer School had been transferred from state support—provided for within the annual budget allocation to the campus—largely to self-support. Through tuition fees the summer session paid its own costs. This change did not handicap San José State University because the summer programs were among the most popular of the state colleges' programs. Operating costs remained low and the state's accounting system did not monitor general fund support migrating into Summer Session administration.

The sufficiency of income actually encouraged the summer recruitment of nationally recognized experts to teach at San José State University. Between the institution of self-support and the implementation of stricter state oversight, state college presidents enjoyed considerable discretion. When the alternative was to return their profits to the state's general fund, the presidents pooled their Summer School profits and losses as a safety net for one another. In the case of San José State University, President MacQuarrie went somewhat further. His judgment determined how much to spend on arts and on attracting star summer faculty. Through the decades in which the program flourished MacQuarrie funded distinguished visitors, performing artists and helped sustain weaker programs at sister campuses. Funds that remained went into the state general fund. The Great Depression impacted this established routine.

During the 1930s Summer School still addressed the needs of public school teachers, its base constituency. Through the first years of the Depression schoolteachers, retaining their jobs amid growing unemployment in the private sector, persevered at summer sessions. As a group, their income remained stable. And, as yet, their need for further education appeared constant. These conditions held amid the devastating employment reductions across the land.

Summer School Director George E. Freeland embraced the self-support concept early in the Depression. By increasing student fees in 1932 to $20 and by attracting 1,016 enrollees, summer school turned a profit of $2,500. Freeland shared his budget calculations with the *Mercury Herald* and maintained, further, that by attracting more than 1,000 teachers to San José, Summer School contributed $225,000 to the depressed local economy. Freeland's logic included the until-then reliable and predictable incomes of the teachers, their need for continuing education and the emerging reality that people (even taxpayers already supporting public education) would pay for the specific educational products that they wanted. As Freeland correctly judged, employed professionals were even willing to pay a little bit more. Freeland's premises remained sound, but changing conditions undermined the conclusion.[23]

The Depression lasted too long and it ran too deep for teachers to escape the economic ravages of the decade. They ceased being the secure and aspiring professionals Freeland's model anticipated. School district curtailments reduced their ranks. They became year-to-year employees, hired all too frequently on opening day of the fall term. In place of pay increases for summer and extension units, pay cuts became endemic. Freeland's 1932 profit became a loss in 1933 when enrollment plummeted. That Depression year became so difficult that the State Department of Finance considered closing Chico, Santa Barbara and Humboldt State Colleges.[24]

When Depression unemployment became wartime over employment the result was the same. Both created insufficient enrollments. As late as 1942, San José State University's summer program remained fragile and discontinuance remained an option. The summer program survived on innovation and administrative resolve.[25]

Early in the war years, Summer School appealed to enrollees by offering speed-up programs so students could complete their degrees before volunteering or being drafted into the military services. Special math courses for those seeking military commissions were offered. Typing, first aid and assorted skills courses emerged to enable housewives to contribute to the expanding war effort. Summer courses prepared ordinary people for home-front jobs in the wartime life of the nation. Rather than closing, Summer School incorporated government-sponsored vocational classes.

The 13-week program packed the summer of 1942 and included four courses in machine shop basics, three courses in ship fitting and another in marine electricity. Women were particularly welcomed and encouraged to sign up for sheet metal and machine shop skills. In fact, the instructors pointed to their superiority to male students in their display of patience, carefulness and manual dexterity. Bulk and strength were unnecessary for skilled machinists. All who successfully completed the courses, female and male students alike, became eligible for immediate employment in the burgeoning local defense plants.

The most innovative feature of the program, however, was not the new courses. Program flexibility best addressed the new national reality. Students could select from three scheduling options: daily from 12:00 noon to 4:00 p.m., evening classes from 4:00 to 8:00 p.m. and night classes from 8:00 p.m. until midnight! Those who held day jobs, even working a swing shift, could enroll in the summer classes and be guaranteed another, perhaps better, job at the end of the program.

Administrative resolve also helped the summer program survive. To boost attendance, President MacQuarrie came close to wrapping the program in the American flag, at least for the public schoolteachers. He wanted the old Summer School base to return to San José State University "…as their contribution to better service in the national emergency."[26]

By then teachers had chosen their own responses to the national emergency. Some joined the military services, some relocated into the growing war industries and some who remained in teaching chose defense-related summer jobs. Summer School, through 1945, ceased being the schoolteacher's primary option.

Victory in Europe and Asia and the collapse, surrender and occupations of Germany and Japan in 1945 dramatically reversed the fortunes of higher education across America. The enactment of the GI Bill by the U.S. Congress represented a grateful nation's "thank you" to the young veterans who served America so nobly in an unquestionably just war. Those who survived and returned converted the national generosity into changed lives and a changed America. Summer School, Continuing Education, regular session, all these were paid for by a nation that stepped from World War II into a reconstituted economy. Free higher education for a generation, pent up savings among defense workers and a robust union labor movement were among the ingredients that converted American society into one with a massive middle class. The 1940s and 1950s propelled this revolutionary economy and the accompanying social changes. Summer School in 1946 represented the first revitalizing wave to reach San José State University.

For the six-week summer session the old mantra sounded again. The first post-war Summer School marked yet another record-breaking enrollment with 1,983 students. That summer 76 completed their bachelors' degrees. A novelty, however, arrived with the veterans. They protested the limited availability of housing and its poor quality.[27]

The summer curriculum reverted to its traditional education orientation with special courses designed for new teachers. Other refresher courses looked to former teachers who were returning to the classroom from military service or from the demobilized war industry. Realizing that all of the veterans were not intent on teaching careers, Summer Session planners broadened the curriculum to include business, humanities and arts, science and mathematics.

Measured in university time, few years passed between the 1940s arrival of the veterans, the 1960s arrival and 1970s departure of their children—the baby boomers. In each case, Summer School rode the crest of the rising numbers, delivered relevant curricula and then retrenched, just like the university. Both surged and ebbed with the tides of demography, economics and social change. The impact of minority protests, educational opportunity, information technology and the high tech boom of the 1990s remained ahead. So too were the innovations of Winter Session, Special Session, eCampus, year-round operations and the end of Summer School as a Continuing Education function.

Chapter Four

What Came First?

Those administrators who presided jointly over Summer School and traditional Continuing Education came to their tasks just as the early schoolteachers came to theirs. They learned by doing. From a modern organization and management perspective, the arrival process was untidy. The activities of Summer School and extension shared basic purposes. As well, they often shared faculty, students, facilities and, in time, they shared an evolving organizational structure. Naturally enough, summer session and extension classes came to share administrators, once such a specialty in academic management arose.

As with programs at other major universities, Continuing Education came to assume the magnitude of an invisible university. Continuing Education learned to do just about everything. In fact, the closest student of the subject, Marcia Salner, concluded that there was only one way to judge what was a continuing education activity rather than a regular college activity. You had to know the answer before asking the question! This extension course labyrinth at San José State University began simply and innocently enough with travel education and science camp. Again, President Morris E. Dailey was the founder of what would evolve into International and Extended Studies. The parallels with his founding of Summer Session end here. For extension he did not involve the trustees and he did not use state funding. Dailey's dual distinction with extension was its founder and first teacher. He inaugurated Continuing Education by personally offering the first course, travel education, during the summer of 1909.

In-Service Education for SJSU Faculty

President Dailey's primary objective was in-service education for his own faculty. His advocacy for sabbatical leaves and his support for multi-year contracts suggest that he viewed his teaching staff as they viewed their students. All teachers need professional development. Scheduling contributed to the president's travel education initiative, too. During the summer of 1909 the campus was to undergo post-earthquake rebuilding. With Summer School canceled, Dailey anticipated no other claim to his official attention.

The president's personality and his personal circumstances, likewise, contributed to this particular educational departure. Dailey was well known for his humor and goodwill.[28] When he organized Continuing Education's first travel summer in Europe, he was 42 years of age. Still a bachelor, he lacked family obligations which otherwise could have restricted his personal participation. His actual leadership of the tour itself illustrated the quaintness of 1909 academic life. Likewise, this steppingstone to modern travel study foreshadowed the quality of future programs.

The digital version of the historic departure photograph reveals the simplicity and the promise of this undertaking. The time was 7:00 a.m. on a clear Saturday morning, June 26, 1909. The place was the rail platform at the Southern Pacific depot located on Market Street in San José. The candid photograph captured the normal school's president and faculty awaiting their boarding call. Behind them was their special car, the "Truckee," which would begin their ambitious three months of study and travel.

BON VOYAGE! MEMBERS OF NORMAL SCHOOL FACULTY ABOUT TO BOARD SPECIAL CAR WHICH WILL START THEM ON JOURNEY TO EUROPE.

—Photo by Tucker.

Faculty and President Dailey ready for departure on the first travel study program, June 26, 1909.

Beginning of International Travel Study

President Dailey, clearly, was in charge. His boater hat, however, mitigated the formality of his dark suit and suggested good times ahead. The traveling party began with 24 and increased en route to 29 members, all but four of whom were the school's women faculty. Those populating the platform photograph were well turned out. Though unimaginable from the perspective of 21st century faculty counterparts, the women wore the cumbersome fashions of the Edwardian era, gowns crowned by immense millinery. In this attire they would entrain for Chicago, Niagara Falls and New York. After crossing America in coach they would connect in New York City to the White Star Line's *Philadelphia* and complete the trans-Atlantic crossing at Antwerp. For their return most of the party scheduled a Liverpool departure on September 9 and then reversed the five-day transcontinental rail journey. For such a full and ambitious summer ahead, the platform party appeared subdued, but undoubtedly it was eager.

The well-filled itinerary included stops at educational and cultural institutions, architectural and historic sites. It included special attention to the renowned galleries and museums that offered the normal school faculty glimpses into worlds beyond their California experiences. En route they visited Belgium, Holland, Germany, Switzerland, Italy, France and England.[29]

Every class enjoys at least one prize student. In the case of Continuing Education's first travel study course she was Estelle Greathead, who distinguished herself as the most accomplished and lastingly productive participant. Her written final report, whether self-assigned or required, is a model of the best in descriptive analysis and travel literature of that time. Within her published essay Greathead maintained her own personal values while allowing a religiously-divided San José newspaper readership to select from among her gracefully presented conclusions. During her visit she reported on government, archaeology, architecture, law, law enforcement, prisons, classical art, fashion, group psychology, individual behavior within social groups, physical beauty, humor, modes of transportation and religion.

After describing in sensitive detail the excitement and splendor of their audience with Pope Pius X, Greathead allowed *San Jose Daily Mercury* readers to select the event's meaning. In so doing, her journalistic subtlety alerted them that other options existed for other readers. The papal audience "was an interesting ceremony," Greathead concluded. "To those of the Catholic faith it was much more. To all it might have meant a spiritual uplift, if looked at in the right way." Most likely, convictions differed as well among her travel study companions.[30]

When Estelle Greathead signed up for the educational summer trip to Europe in 1909 she had already enjoyed a secured association with the normal school. A graduate of the school, she had been a faculty member for four years. From the start she distinguished herself in teaching and, thereafter, as college registrar. Her final and most enduring service to San José State University was her early history of the school, *The Story of an Inspiring Past*, published by the college in 1928.

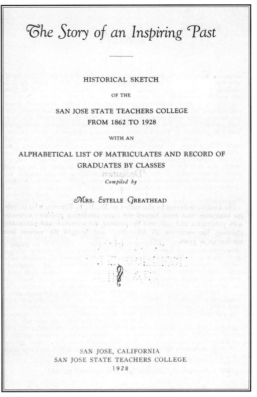

Estelle Greathead

The Story of an Inspiring Past title page.

Perhaps compelled by modesty, Greathead paused in her text only so briefly on the memorable and historic summer of 1909. Its mention, however, establishes extension's early contribution to her academic development. More completely, her travel essay documents the founding of Continuing Education as distinct from Summer School. In composing and publishing her analysis, Greathead established the standard to which Continuing Education aspires.

Continuing Education and Field Studies in Natural History

In the summer of 1931 seven science faculty members from San José State Teachers College enrolled students for a single week course, charged tuition, conducted instruction and awarded academic credits. The driving purpose was compatible with accepted continuing education goals. The target clientele was elementary school teachers, too many of whom taught science without having studied it. What better way to rectify this deficiency, particularly at the end of an arduous school year? What made this continuing education course particularly attractive to the wearied teachers was that the instruction took place in the field, first at Big Basin Redwoods State Park in Santa Cruz County.

West Coast School of Nature Study 1936 schedule of classes.

Fortunately, two professors within the second generation (1940s) of what was known as West Coast Nature School's leadership knew the program's origins and recorded their recollections. Biologist G. A. "Bill" McCallum summarized

the school's history as a retirement retrospective in 1976. He was the first participant-observer to document the relationship of West Coast Nature School to Continuing Education.

Journalism Professor Dwight Bentel taught photography at the nature school and advanced McCallum's story in 1992. He gathered and first published an early account of Nature Studies and Extended Education. For Bentel's article, "When Field Studies in Natural History Goes to Death Valley" go to www.ies.sjsu.edu/history/death-valley-article.

G. A. "Bill" McCallum

By beginning in 1931 the nature school did not predate the organization of Continuing Education, which was already functioning, with or without a sophisticated management structure. In the fall of 1925, San José State University opened classes to the public, non-students and non-teachers. As in the Open University program of a half-century later, the non-matriculated students could register if they had the consent of the instructor and paid the fee, in that day $1.50.

These designated courses, which predated nature studies, ranged from interior decorating and professional education to those supporting general education—science, psychology and American history. Professor James C.

Dwight Bentel

DeVoss team-taught a regular class opened to extension students. He and Dr. Dorothy Hazeltine Yates offered a course in problems in modern psychology. These two, with George E. Freeland from education, were among the early faculty who taught in an established program for Continuing Education.[31]

Thus, President Dailey founded modern Continuing Education by establishing its major steppingstone, travel study, in 1909. Next came DeVoss, Yates and Freeland who functioned in an organized program in 1925. Then followed Field Studies in Natural History in 1931. The oddity within this organizational development was that the nature studies program, embedded in the science departments, operated independently of higher administrative authority or management.

San José State University Science Building, c. 1940.

The organization of the California State College System in 1960, however, created a statewide administrative bureaucracy that chose to address such a major irregularity. A unit that functioned like continuing education simply had to be organized under a campus Office of Continuing Education.[32]

President John T. Wahlquist, under duress from the Chancellor's Legal Affairs Office, turned to Joe H. West, dean of Educational Services and Summer Sessions and a master of campus diplomacy. West reconciled the conflicting perspectives. The West Coast School of Nature Studies became Field Studies in Natural History. The chair of the Science Education Department became authorized to appoint the directors. The standing committee, consisting of the veteran participants from the science departments, would continue to run the program. One unit of academic credit was authorized for one week in the field. And under extension services management the fee was standardized at $20 per unit.

Financial management was complicated, however. Tuition fees went to Educational Services. Costs for food, insurance and incidental Death Valley expenses went to the College Foundation and the scientists kept the Bank of America account that they earmarked for student scholarships. Despite the financial awkwardness, or probably because of it, the dean of Educational Services secured general agreement. This transition paved the way for Field Studies in Natural History to become the longest-functioning program among Continuing Education's abundant list of modern offerings.

Integrating Continuing Education into SJSU

Dean Joe H. West was the second permanent administrator to carry that title for Educational Services and Summer Sessions. He was the one, though, who defined the boundaries of the early office. Besides talent, his success sprang, in part, from his comfortable association with all university administrators, with faculty and with many students. He viewed Continuing Education as a part of the college and he worked to make it as interactive with the rest of the institution as he could.

Joe H. West

M. Edd Burton

Associate Academic Vice President M. Edd Burton followed McCallum and Bentel as a Death Valley participant-historian. In capturing its visual dimension, Burton became the program's third chronicler. His photography offers insight into the strength of the mythology that enveloped students, teachers and nature. For Field Studies in Natural History photos of Death Valley, go to www.ies.sjsu.edu/history/death-valley-photos.

Field Studies in Natural History participants in Death Valley.

Chapter Five

Leadership Lineage

The founders of public education in Gold Rush California arrived from New England and New York. George W. Minns had been born into a Boston family in 1813. His father, Thomas Minns, an educated man and a newspaper publisher, sent George to private and public schools. The young man responded positively. As the recipient of the Franklin Medal from Boylston Grammar School, George earned the rare privilege of dining at Boston's Faneuil Hall in the company of the city

George W. Minns, 1857–1862

fathers. Thereafter, he earned the bachelor's degree at Harvard College (1836) and then his law degree, again at Harvard (1840). One of Minns' professors was Oliver Wendell Holmes. James Russell Lowell, a fellow student, remained a friend through life.

Although Minns was an excellent student, his degree progress suffered an enforced two-year interruption for a disciplinary infraction: exploding gunpowder in the dormitory. Reinstated, he augmented his classical and legal studies with a personal interest in science, an unofficial minor through which he would later advance teacher preparation in California.

Minns' introduction to in-service education came early and personally. His education at Harvard's Howard Dane Law School blended study of the law with observation of its practice. His mentor was the noted orator Rufus Choate. Admitted to the bar in 1841, Minns pursued his legal career in Suffolk County, then relocated his practice to San Francisco in 1855. Fate intervened, however, in the form of a major career change at age 42.

Minns' arrival in Gold Rush California coincided with a major downturn in the local economy, one that settled into the depression of 1855. He abandoned law and turned to education. He responded to an opening at Union Grammar School and accepted a teaching position there in natural sciences. Among the best educated Californians, Minns became an effective teacher, a popular outside lecturer and an advocate of teaching as a profession.

Minns' combination of education, energy and commitment associated him with the like-minded professionals with whom he collaborated in the creation of public education in California. A pioneer in the field, Minns initiated public higher education in the state by directing Minns' Evening Normal School. The night school's purpose was to upgrade the teaching skills and subject matter competence of employed schoolteachers. Minns also served as the second principal of the California State Normal School, 1865–1866.

Morris Dailey's name recognition within modern Silicon Valley stems from the San José State University auditorium, the memorial that his bereaved colleagues chose for him following his untimely death in 1919. Student and faculty generations since—by hearing, reading and writing his name—preserved Dailey from the historical fate of his numerous contemporaries. In this case, the enduring testimonial is appropriate.

Dailey came to California from the Midwest. Born in Indiana in 1867, he was educated there and in Iowa. He earned two bachelor's degrees and a master's degree. Drake University, the source of one

Morris E. Dailey, 1900–1919

B.S., conferred an honorary doctorate of laws upon him in 1901, the year after he commenced his San José State University presidency.

California's attraction drew the young educator to San José in 1894 where he first taught mathematics. When he returned to San José State University, then a normal school, in 1899 following his graduate work, Dailey became professor of history and vice president. The next year the trustees ousted President James McNaughton and replaced him with Dailey. Well enough educated for the time, his great strengths were his youth, his energy, his democratic spirit, his dedication to his students and to a sense of community service.

At the turn of the 20th century his step up to a normal school presidency was not too great a stretch for a person of his caliber. As an outgoing, engaging and energetic bachelor, Dailey was committed to an educator's life. He was only 33 years old and he enjoyed the work that he undertook. In his days, when the scope of the institution was capable of being understood and managed by one person, Dailey taught classes, encouraged the students, supported the faculty, shared and implemented his vision and enveloped the college in the community. He was the president who gathered unto himself what were to become two distinct roles: the campus academic manager and the institution's representative to the community. Dailey, affectionately known to his faculty as "The Big Chief," was the perfect Mr. Inside and Mr. Outside.

Prominent among the accomplishments of his lengthy presidency was the creation of the first summer session among the California state normal schools. The selection of this particular option, among others, for San José State University to serve the best interests of education statewide was particularly apt. Dailey's motivation for reinventing continuing education in the form of summer travel study seemed multiple. He may have just wanted the sort of good time that a person of his position, disposition and culture would enjoy. The earthquake of 1906 aborted his European holiday and compelled his return to San José. Three years later, in the summer of 1909, the campus was to be under reconstruction, thus no Summer School, so he organized and led a faculty summer abroad.

In the history of San José State University Continuing Education, Dailey identified and began its greatest success. He also put in place a major steppingstone.

Untimely deaths played their part in Continuing Education's history. The movement's early driving force, President Morris Dailey, died unexpectedly while on vacation in Pacific Grove in 1919. His early demise at age 52 ushered in a period of frequent administrative changes within a very short period of years.

Rather than creating instability, presidential musical chairs actually added very measurably to the progress and the success of the college overall. Dr. William W. Kemp, an expert on academic administration, accepted appointment for

William W. Kemp, 1920–1923

the purpose of seeing San José State University through its transition from normal school to teachers college.

Alexander R. Heron, Summer 1923

Mr. Alexander R. Heron, a powerful and adept financial and institutional manager in both government and industry, sustained Summer School and clarified the future role of teacher education in California. Kemp and Heron were abundantly experienced, self-assured experts who took time from their ongoing, dynamic careers and played brief but critical parts in San José State University Continuing Education's development. Their vision was for the complete institution and its place in the advancing design of California life. California as a frontier had passed. California as its own civilization was yet to come. Kemp and Heron facilitated the transition. They understood continuing education, but it was not their primary focus. They were leaders with broader visions.

San José State University centennial historian Benjamin F. Gilbert ranked Dr. Edwin R. Snyder even higher as a contributor to educational advancement. In Snyder's case his vision and propulsion had a practical spin. A highly theoretical person, Snyder developed a philosophy that integrated manual training, fine arts, culture and applications to the industrial and economic life of California. His areas of contribution were many and they had impact: nine years of service as the first state commissioner of industrial and vocational education, his publications, influence on vocational teacher education and the improvement of the California polytechnic

Edwin R. Snyder, 1923–1925

school and his drafting of legislative enactments within the field of vocational education. Gilbert considered Snyder's career to have been vital in California's transition from frontier state to the industrial giant it became. The tangible steppingstone was state industrial expansion in support of World War I production. Throughout Snyder's broad career San José State University was his home base. Continuing education, as lifelong learning, served as one means to his vocational ends.

Like Dailey, Snyder's career concluded early. He also died at age 52, following a two-month illness.

Herman F. Minssen, 1925–1927

The organization man who kept the teachers teaching and the students learning during this segmented interregnum between career presidents was Mr. Herman F. Minssen. He knew San José State University from the classroom up and from the president's office down. He served as teacher, professor and chair of mathematics. He understood the overall functioning of San José State University and Continuing Education through his financial oversight functions. He acted for the president, then served as president until the

permanent appointment of Dr. Thomas W. MacQuarrie in 1927.

Dr. George E. Freeland was a person of talent and capacity whose interests focused on education, but were not contained by the field's parameters. He joined the faculty in 1921 as professor of education and director of teacher training. He moved naturally into a management capacity for Summer Session and Continuing Education. He already possessed the list of degrees that later were

George E. Freeland, 1925–1936

to become the requirements for college appointments. In his case they were the A.B., A.M. and Ph.D. As well, he was experienced in the classroom and at supervision of student teachers.

Freeland was well published, a novelty then. By 1923 he taught Summer School and by the spring of 1925 he managed it. The precise year in which he assumed his management duties in Continuing Education is unclear, but it was well before 1933. For whatever reason, his annual pay records included summer, but not extension, income. Freeland's surviving 1933 report to President MacQuarrie assumed already agreed-upon procedures that he projected into the future operations of Continuing Education.

Naturally enough post-World War I expansion of summer school and continuing education courses prompted the creation of a management structure separate from the president's office. Dr. Freeland was an ideal choice. He possessed paper qualifications, practical experience and related well with the clientele. The education professor had an established network. He placed student teachers into the school districts throughout Northern California and the Central Valley. He traveled around to see them, their master teachers and the school principals. Also, Freeland needed the income supplement. His wife was ill and he had five dependents.

Freeland's most significant contribution to the recorded history of Continuing Education is the annual report that he presented to President MacQuarrie in 1933. Its most striking feature, at least from a 21st century perspective, is that the report was gratuitous. It is the professor's written recapitulation of what must have been a verbal understanding. The document reveals that San José State University extension classes were offered as far away as Watsonville, Santa Cruz, Merced, Modesto, Sacramento, Woodland, Lodi, Stockton and Tracy. Because schoolteacher salaries were being reduced and because other normal schools were competing at lower prices, Freeland recommended that San José State University reduce its continuing education fees from six dollars to four dollars per semester.

Freeland's report stunner was the revelation of how the money was managed. The students, or the local school superintendent, paid continuing education fees to a Mrs. Latta, who was subordinate to Dr. Freeland. She held the money in a non-state bank account, paid the expenses of the program and conveyed the remainder to Freeland as his remuneration. This was the verbal agreement between the San José State University president and the director of Continuing Education as of 1933.

As the Great Depression exacted its toll upon Continuing Education and Summer School, Freeland resigned his appointment and focused his energies on professional writing. Over the next decade he published eight books in social studies and education that went through 24 printings. His New York publisher was Scribner's. Meanwhile, the programs went into Depression-induced decline.

Thomas W. MacQuarrie, 1936–1941

Dr. Thomas W. MacQuarrie was the best-prepared educator to have been selected to lead San José State University up to that time. His academic credentials set the standard for future permanent appointments. In his case the credentials sparkled. The list began with a four-year diploma from the Wisconsin State Normal in 1900. As an army major at the end of World War I, MacQuarrie studied psychological testing in Kings College, London. At Stanford University, after the war, MacQuarrie earned an A.B., M.A. and Ph.D. in four years, during which time he earned membership in Phi Beta Kappa. His revised dissertation became a standard evaluation tool for counselors and personnel officers. Its English, German and Spanish editions exceeded one million copies. His management experience included intermittent appointments at all levels of education and within the Veterans' Bureau.

To acquire his services, the State Department of Education set aside the worthy applications of George E. Freeland, Herman F. Minssen and another solid, on-campus administrator. MacQuarrie's personal warmth sealed the decision. The mix of qualifications and circumstances resulted in the longest presidential administration in San José State University history, 1927–1952. MacQuarrie tangibly advanced San José State University through the Roaring Twenties, the Great Depression, World War II and GI Bill enrollment explosions. His focus was on education for careers. His impact was upon program diversification and expansion.

At first Summer Session and Continuing Education were the easy parts. MacQuarrie wisely retained the services of Herman F. Minssen by returning him as vice president. Minssen commanded the financial structure of the college, with Summer School operations included. Enduring friendship among the MacQuarries and Minssens may be assumed from the twilight marriage of widower MacQuarrie and Edith Minssen, widow of Herman F. Minssen.

Summer School and Continuing Education operations continued under the management of George E. Freeland until his resignation in 1936. Freeland's management was sound, but the economy was to collapse. The casual informality of Freeland's memo report of 1933 demonstrates that neither Minssen nor MacQuarrie intruded into program management. Program shrinkage induced by the Depression and Freeland's resignation returned seriously reduced programs to the oversight of the president's office. There it became an add-on activity for MacQuarrie and those few he might interest in such an additional assignment—largely uncompensated.

Professor William H. Poytress never directed Continuing Education, but he always offered a willing hand to President MacQuarrie. This was particularly true during the bridge years of the Depression and World War II. An economist who headed the social science department, "Wild Bill" Poytress enjoyed his teaching days. So did his students, once they discovered that his bombast would not hamper their grades. Three years after his retirement, students selected their favorite professor to be the grand marshal for homecoming. To their delight and to his, too, Poytress partook of all the hoopla at

William H. Poytress, 1936–1941

Spartan Stadium. President MacQuarrie liked Poytress, too. He had a quick mind, public appeal and he always showed up when others faded away. Poytress shared his celebrity with a suffering Continuing Education. He was a public advance man for Summer Session. He was the most sought after director of professional and commercial gatherings as well as an after-dinner speaker. His high-profile extension presentations were regularly mentioned in the press. MacQuarrie even used Poytress to jolly up the faculty and student body while updating them on critical world events and their impact on the home front during World War II.

During the period of ebbing fortunes and with no dedicated leadership the programs subsisted out of the president's office and remained alive through the generous compulsions of faculty members such as Mr. William H. Poytress.

Joe H. West, 1942–1947, 1954–1965

Joe H. West's unduplicated record in San José State University administrative history included two separate terms as director of Continuing Education. Barely recommended by a 1925 A.B. from New Mexico State Teachers College and a 1927 M.A. from Stanford University, West advanced his career through application of remarkable talent and diplomacy. His work ethic and his unfailing sense of humor helped, too. This unblemished string of career successes began with his 1929 appointment as assistant registrar and continued until his retirement in 1965. The primary list included these: Registrar, dean of students, dean of Educational Services and Summer School (twice) and acting dean of the college (comparable to the modern provost). His first extension service was an assignment in addition to his full-time position as registrar. His service as dean of the college was in addition to his full-time position as dean of Educational Services and Summer Session.

When asked where he spent most of his time when he held two important jobs, the dean of deans responded, "in the corridor between the two offices." Why, with all his success, did he want to retire? "When they begin talking about tearing down buildings constructed since you came...." Humor was not the reason why Presidents MacQuarrie, John T. Wahlquist and Robert D. Clark valued West.

His judgements and his advice on college problems, offered only upon request, were astute and always apt. For MacQuarrie he resuscitated extension and maintained it on life support until the GI Bill could restore good health and renew growth. For Wahlquist he accepted the deanship, stabilized and advanced Summer School and Continuing Education into the modern era. His management received commendations for high quality and balanced budgets. At the conclusion of his career Dean West provided his quietest, most confidential service to his final president.

Robert Clark wanted to remold the college administration and in so doing remove tradition-bound administrators. His reorganization scheme itself would eject those Clark considered least progressive. The case of librarian Joyce Backus was unique, though. Miss Backus, as she insisted on being called, was appointed back in 1923 and, thus, was senior even to West. Further, she enjoyed a "status" appointment that had been phased out, but still prevented her mandatory retirement because of age. Highly directive in her style, she found it difficult to change with the long evolution of the college. Clark thought that her concept of library management seemed to better fit the teachers college she joined in 1923 than the university Clark intended to create in 1965. Because Dean West's management responsibilities included the library, Clark asked West to get Backus to retire, even though she did not have to or wish to do so. After all, wasn't West the dean of deans—diplomatic, charming and convincing?

San José State University legend has West smiling broadly, telling the new president that his plan would not work. But because West always did his best, he would try. Well, when West suggested her retirement, Miss Backus became so outraged at him that she summarily resigned.

Contained within West's long-archived personnel action file is a thick petition from the 1960s. It justifies to the Office of the Chancellor why a campus building, Joe West Hall, should skirt system policy and be named after a person still living. All of West's fine achievements were documented, but for his final service for President Clark. Clark was fortunate that the college's unevolved administrative structure still made the dean of Educational Services and Summer Sessions responsible for the library.

Raymond M. Mosher, 1948–1953

Raymond M. Mosher was a local product. Born in Palo Alto in 1894, he attended high school there. Next, he enrolled at San José State Normal School where he studied and taught from 1913 until World War I intervened. After serving as a private in the medical corps (158th Field Hospital Company, 115th Sanitary Train) he entered Stanford University where he earned his A.B. in 1919 and M.A. in 1922. He completed his Ph.D. in 1926 at Columbia University.

Young Mosher was a proficient pianist and initially explored a career in music education. In fact, in 1930 President MacQuarrie attempted to recruit him from the University of Idaho to head the university music department. Mosher's research interests, however, were changing his concerns from how students learned music to how students learned.

The following year, 1931, he accepted MacQuarrie's alternate offer, to head the psychology department. Mosher promptly organized the department into its modern configuration. He eliminated philosophy and constructed a curriculum in harmony with the emerging professional fields of the discipline. He recruited faculty members who were experts within each of the specializations. The teacher specialists then pursued professional agendas within their domains that would grow into major funded research.

Mosher's administrative talents prompted President MacQuarrie to sound him out for the position of the first full-time director of Summer Session and Extension Services. West was re-developing the program, and by the spring of 1948 it required fully dedicated management. Also, West deserved consideration, one job at a time.

President MacQuarrie recognized Mosher's skills and contributions to Continuing Education, but also accepted the reality of his larger career opportunities. MacQuarrie authorized the chancellor of the University of Montana to include Mosher in an early presidential search. In 1953 Mosher took temporary leave from Continuing Education to accept the acting presidency of Eastern Washington College of Education. The opportunity ended poorly, though. Terminally ill, Mosher returned to his home in the William Street Park neighborhood and a large funeral at St. Patrick's Church on East Santa Clara Street. During the short interval, new President John T. Wahlquist had protected Mosher and advanced Continuing Education. In a compassionate note to Mosher, Wahlquist retained him at the top faculty rank, but with special assignment to his own office. Wahlquist's unstated intent was that Mosher's dwindling capacities determined his workload. At the same time Wahlquist moved West into the increasingly important position of dean of Educational Services and Summer Session.

William G. Sweeney, 1953–1954

William G. Sweeney offered a cameo appearance in the history of Continuing Education, one that came early in his remarkable career in professional education. He served a single interim year, the leave time during which Dean Raymond M. Mosher was acting president at Eastern Washington College of Education. Sweeney's selection as interim dean by a new president, Wahlquist, suggests that his reputation preceded him. The ever-present and attentive West belonged to Wahlquist's campus advisory council and undoubtedly was consulted.

But for his single year directing Summer Session and Continuing Education, Sweeney spent an entire career in the education department and school. His association with the college preceded his faculty appointment. Sweeney was a local boy. Born in 1908, he attended San Jose High School and matriculated to San José State University where he earned his bachelor's degree in 1930. The master's degree followed at Stanford in 1934. Sweeney's doctorate in education, also from Stanford, lingered until 1942. He had been teaching full time at San José State University since 1934. As with California teachers generally, he advanced his education as he could, on the job. During the war years he lent a glad hand to William H. Poytress trying to maintain Summer School. By 1949 he headed the education department that initiated audiovisual services. When that department evolved into a college-wide function, its campus management gravitated to Continuing Education.

Perhaps distracted by his impending call to the Washington presidency, Dean Mosher did not host any campus celebration for the 50th anniversary of Summer School in 1953. Better late than never, Sweeney marked the birthday, belatedly, in 1954, during his brief chance to serve the cause of Continuing Education.

Sweeney retired as dean of education in 1971. The education building was renamed in his honor for having presided over the immense changes in his field.

The faculty grew from 12 educators to 100 and they produced the most elementary schoolteachers of any college in the West. Sweeney consistently served this core clientele throughout his career.

At the start of the 21st century, San José State University students knew Joe West as a high-rise dorm, one that lived on in the shadow of the even higher-rise Campus Village. For senior emeritus faculty to recall West or his work, absentmindedness helps. Through four decades too much has changed: the titles, the functions, the organizations and even the reality. Joe H. West served as dean of Educational Services and Summer Session from 1954–1965. Like many other retirees Joe and Dorothy West took their leave by promptly closing their family home in Willow Glen and relocating with their dog, Pooh, to Sun City, California. West's enduring satisfactions included the fact that he left every office he had occupied and every program he had managed in pristine condition.

Leo P. Kibby, 1965–1970

Leo P. Kibby capped his 24-year career of history teaching and departmental level administration with a successful five-year appointment as dean of Educational Services and Summer Session. Dean West handed him a well-functioning program, resting upon well-designed management procedures. Kibby recognized success when he received it and added some enhancements of his own. He conducted sample surveys of the changing interests of summer students. He began year-round planning with group meetings followed with his individual consultations among the department chairmen and the deans. He explained clearly and in writing the exact financial requirements of the program. He restated for new participants in Summer School what the general underpinnings of the successful program were. He admonished the department chairs not to extract any administrative time if they chose to teach.

His own educational background was one that President Wahlquist chose to downplay – degrees mostly from California and other western universities. Born in

Kansas, Kibby had grown up in California's Central Valley. He earned the A.B. from Stanford University in 1929 and the A.M. from New Mexico State Teachers College in 1933. He received the Ph.D. from the University of Southern California during World War II in 1942. Kibby considered United States history as his field and the Civil War as his scholarly specialty. He enjoyed a modest run of publications during the concluding decade of his career, the 1960s.

When President MacQuarrie recruited Kibby in 1946, the press was on. War veterans had already appeared in large numbers for Summer School and an avalanche created by the GI Bill was to start. Kibby accepted an associate professorship, a mid-range appointment indicating the strength of Kibby's degrees and experience meeting MacQuarrie's need. Kibby's job performance earned him quick promotion to full professor of history and political science in 1950. Two years later, the president named him head of the Social Science Department. From then until his appointment as dean in 1965, Kibby endured five different reorganizations and title changes, all at the hands of the college president and none with any significant advancement.

Dean West, who occasionally nominated successors to positions he vacated, participated in the college's upper echelon personnel decisions. He, of course, knew Kibby and the quality of his work through years of Summer School and Extension Services coordination. What he saw was an effective administrator who was competent, reliable and thorough. He never went home until all of the day's work was carefully dispatched from his desk. When Paul M. Bradley (future acting dean of Continuing Education) came to work as his assistant, Kibby's predictability extended to the next day's arrival time and what tasks would be addressed then and by his action calendar.

Kibby was a gentleman of the old school. He always dressed as a professor and a dean might then be expected to dress. He was a family man and particularly proud of his children. Humor was hardly his strongest feature, but it did exist. When his wife and her twin sister appeared together the dean would introduce them as "my wives." Strangers hardly knew how to respond. Friends and acquaintances enjoyed the laugh and enjoyed the dean.

The ideal dean for the period, Leo T. Kibby did not fiddle with success. He managed it perfectly and enhanced Summer Session and Continuing Education under improving conditions. At his elbow was the heir apparent, Associate Dean Ralph C. Bohn.

Ralph C. Bohn, 1970–1992

Given the status of San José State University's recorded history, Ralph C. Bohn is the second-longest serving administrator in the history of the institution. Bohn occupied a single office, dean of Continuing Education, for 22 years. Counting his two years as Dean Kibby's assistant, his total approaches, but does not quite reach, the 25 year career record of SJSU President Thomas W. MacQuarrie (1927–1952).

Dean Bohn was energetic, bright and efficient from the start. He quickly enough earned all of his degrees (B.S., 1950; M.Ed., 1954; and Ed.D., 1957) from the same university, Wayne State in Nebraska. His academic field was industrial arts, but it failed to contain his energy. Bohn was a program developer, a type A personality who thrived on making things run right. His long-term associate and successor, Dr. Paul M. Bradley, felt that the only thing Bohn never figured out was retirement. As a consultant in retirement, the former dean continued doing what he always did, only worldwide and on his own travel schedule.

In office, Bohn's problems were Continuing Education's problems. His solutions impacted the larger environment in which Continuing Education lived. The cyclical demise of the schoolteacher clientele and the rise of local competitors depreciated the value of the Continuing Education Unit (CEU) credit. Competing programs fought over fewer students by granting more credit for less work.

Bohn's solution to the problem of too much credit being lavished upon too little course work began with the system of accrediting the credit-granting institutions. He joined WASC, the Western Association of Schools and Colleges, and became active in its enforcement. His intent was to end credit devaluation. Over time he succeeded by having this sensitive area of college activity specifically included in new WASC accreditation criteria.

On campus, Bohn worked with everyone who had an interest to change noncredit courses from the University Foundation to his domain. Then, with Bradley, he broadened Summer Session to Special Session and thus converted Continuing Education into a year-round institution. Special Session courses, determined by the chairs and deans, received regular university credit. Continuing Education offered noncredit courses that grew with the professional development needs of technology workers who gathered to Silicon Valley. For years, the workforce of Silicon Valley swelled Continuing Education enrollments as employers paid or reimbursed employees to improve their careers with noncredit professional development courses, making San José State University one of the top two or three CSU programs annually.

University presidents came and went during Bohn's decades. He reported to academic vice presidents, his first and last being the most firmly established in their offices. Bohn and Academic Vice President Hobert W. Burns worked well together. The two largely agreed on campus priorities and the vice president always knew where to go when he needed additional funding. Burns, however, did not press Bohn excessively and did not intrude into a well-managed program. A new relationship between the departments and colleges and Continuing Education emerged and reshaped Continuing Education. Degree credit programs in Special Session grew and noncredit programs were overshadowed by more and different programs in the 1960s–1990s. Bohn and his final boss, Academic Vice President Arlene Okerlund, did not always agree on the issues. Simultaneously, the deans always seemed to want more money from Continuing Education. It seemed that everyone else did, too. Bohn, tired of the routine, retired to his oceanfront home, but could not just watch the Pacific. He took on projects for the chancellor's office, foreign universities and more.

A different route brought Paul M. Bradley to San José State University Continuing Education. In 1968 he tired of working for a truck company in Eureka, California and headed south. His objective, a career in public administration, brought him to San José where he became the first responder to Dean Kibby's ad for a different job, administrative assistant. Kibby's problem was that he was unclear what an administrative assistant should do. The two highly personable men, one concluding a career and the other commencing one, chatted first and then formalized the job requirements and responsibilities. When the line of applicants appeared, each interviewed against the Kibby-Bradley matrix. Needless to say, Bradley received the appointment.

Paul M. Bradley, 1992–1996

Bradley liked the work and liked Kibby, whom he considered a respectable, efficient and good person. Bradley turned out reports and budgets and dabbled in early marketing; things he had done in Eureka. Sharon Cancilla arrived in 1969 and addressed the increasing workload, too. Bradley moved on to brochures and later into policy matters with Bohn. Cancilla also advanced, from staff to program management.

Bradley retained his high regard for Kibby. Besides being efficient he was kindly—even "fatherly, no, grandfatherly," according to Bradley. Before retiring "Kibby sat me down and said, 'Son, you need an advanced degree'" in this business. So, Bradley completed an M.A. at San José State University. In time Bohn told him the same thing. Like Kibby, Bradley said, "This time it was, 'Son, you need a doctorate.'" So, Bradley took leave from a supportive college and earned the Ph.D. in Higher Education at the University of Washington.

Once Bradley had the doctorate, Bohn moved him up into more responsible positions until he became associate dean. No official title existed as director of Summer Session, but that was Bradley's major function for years. He served as acting dean for a semester when Bohn was away and then for a year when Bohn took a sabbatical leave. At Dean Bohn's retirement in 1992, Bradley again accepted the top management position. This time his acting deanship lasted an unprecedented four and a half years, ending with the appointment of Dean Mark Novak.

Through the years Bradley pursued a hobby that undoubtedly helped him retain the quiet charm that he and Kibby shared in their 1968 interview. His restored classic automobiles always called for inspection and happy chatter at special campus events.

For the first time in its history, in 1996, San José State University recruited an experienced professional in the field of continuing education. The program was fully established, sound and faced a potentially exciting and rewarding future of service in Silicon Valley and beyond. The selectors came up short in their 1995 search, but met their own leadership criteria the following year. Their model was an accomplished academic with sufficient experience so that the complexities of curriculum, personnel, finance, marketing and development would not have to be learned on the job. Equally important, the successful candidate should not be too encumbered. An innovative and successful future at San José State University was the goal.

Dr. Mark Novak was born in New Jersey and obtained his B.A. from Rutgers University in 1969. In record time, four years, he completed the Ph.D. at York University in Toronto, Ontario. The Canadian attraction was the vibrancy of a new university with a fresh program in sociology. On arrival Novak discovered another plus, a distinctly international quality to the student body that broadened his perspective as a sociologist and as a person.

Mark Novak, 1996–2006

Rather than returning home with his new doctorate, Novak accepted a faculty position in the sociology department at University of Winnipeg. There he learned his basic trade. He taught and students learned. Young and energetic, Novak regularly offered continuing education courses and began an ongoing publishing career in sociology.

Major change took place in 1989 when he accepted the associate dean's post for Continuing Education at the University of Manitoba. This decision brought with it the structured life of administration, being in the office and suited up every day to manage a staff and advance a program with a distinct bottom line. He discovered the difference between fulfilling self-support budget expectations and accomplishing instructional objectives.

Between 1989 and 1996 he participated in all aspects of continuing education and the relevant professional associations. Both internal management, including finance and accounting, and the need to meet the public out in the community became his particular concerns. With success came the natural progression to a deanship while still in mid-career. He chose San José State University rather than a tempting, simultaneous offer to return to Rutgers. The Novaks wished to move forward rather than return to where they had been.

The easiest adjustment was trading the forty-degree below zero winters for the California experience. More challenging was the collapse of the dot.com boom and with it the professional development market. In their place Novak grew an international program and tapped the vast potential of distance learning. To institutionalize the innovations of technology, Novak hired a new breed of instructional specialists who guided resident faculty in placing their redesigned instruction before a virtual eCampus clientele and acquired an in-house Web designer to create and administer a growing international online presence.

This "design by delivery" online instructional system liberated Continuing Education from the restrictions of time and place. Novak saw this as just one of the multiple ways San José State University's modern programs extended access through unlimited innovation.

Most recent Continuing Education leadership—Paul Bradley, left, Mark Novak, center and Ralph Bohn.

Chapter Six

The Price of Success

A probing analysis, *Continuing Education in the California State University*, appeared in 1988. Marcia Salner of Consulting Services in Education wrote the book and the California State University Office of the Chancellor published it. The work's integrity is evident throughout, particularly in the concluding "Epilogue" where Salner summarized the unhappy and deeply threatened condition of continuing education statewide. After decades of Chancellor Glenn S. Dumke's inspired vision and intense systematization at the hands of his greatly expanded staff, continuing education stared into a beckoning abyss. The standard success formula of centralized leadership, abundant resources, vision, consultation and action converted campus accomplishment into system failure.[33]

Structural, Fiscal Changes

California's Master Plan for Higher Education, adopted in 1960, organized the largely independent state colleges into the new California State College System. The Office of the Chancellor established itself in Long Beach, California and repositioned the fulcrum of power. Decision-making authority became centralized and remote.

When Chancellor Dumke translated his vision for California education into his action plan in 1971, he gave a high priority to in-service professional education. The bedrock of the state master plan—California's promise of free public higher education to all who were capable of profiting from it—was Dumke's point of departure. Unfortunately, economics and altered public sentiment were simultaneously creating a new environment. Campus disorders, Proposition 13 tax limitations and constricted budgets for higher education had already impacted public policy. And even though California's noble commitment remained on the books, its strength eroded within legislative finance committees. Thus, Continuing Education at San José State University and throughout the California system found itself positioned between the chancellor's enhanced goals for adult higher education and the legislature's resolve not to finance what those goals required. The impact on Continuing Education was substantial, especially in the realm of finance where the struggles became focused.

During better economic times the state legislature had revised its historic policy of claiming for the state's general fund all profits from campus continuing education operations. After 1967 each campus retained 75 percent of its own self-generated revenues. The chancellor's office, for its part, received 25 percent of the revenues of all campuses combined. These accounts constituted the Continuing Education Revenue Funds (CERF). Interest-bearing and growing, they resided in the continuing education program at each campus and in the chancellor's office. The fund's purpose was to protect continuing education programs during cyclical downturns and to provide start-up costs for program innovations. To this fund Chancellor Dumke turned in order to implement his vision of accessible higher education for working adults.[34]

Dumke's plan was a major departure from the status quo and addressed what study groups and the state legislature itself identified as the remaining unmet need in California higher education under the master plan of 1960. Propelled by Chancellor Dumke's leadership, his staff advanced with varying degrees of support from the campus presidents and deans of continuing education. The result was their creation of the Consortium of State Colleges and Universities.

CSU Consortium

Popularly known as the 1,000-Mile Campus, the consortium, besides being expensive to manage, became coordination, articulation and committee-intensive. Its intent was to convert all of the individual campuses into one seamless educational structure that would encourage career mobile adults to acquire academic degrees, unimpeded by programmatic idiosyncrasies among the campuses. Students were never to miss an educational step as their career opportunities drew them around California.

Well, for a vision dependent upon the solvency of the Continuing Education Revenue Fund, its problems multiplied. Among them were rising costs, low enrollments, flawed accounting and the legislature's decision simply to not fund higher education for adults who were already employed. Also, the attenuating management and financial fallout associated with the impending collapse of the consortium threatened the interests of campus continuing education programs. That, generally, was the view from the campus deans.

San José State University's Dean of Continuing Education Dr. Ralph C. Bohn assumed the task of delivering the fateful message to the consortium and to its sponsor, the chancellor's office. His delivery occasion was well timed and followed an embarrassing announcement concerning the beleaguered consortium. An audit imploded a projected surplus and revealed a $700,000 operating deficit, one that was expected to double by the following year, 1987. Bohn fixed responsibility for the operating deficit at the chancellor's office. Citing system policy, he maintained that the chancellor's office was required to repay—with interest—the "loan" from the Continuing Education Revenue Fund being used to cover the deficit.[35]

As the consortium moved from life to death, unfunded by the legislature and arguably exceeding the system's own resources, the chancellor's new departure failed. And with this failure, continuing education descended into the most troubled period in its history. Centralized leadership of the largest institution of public higher education had identified a noble cause only to overextend a system, one whose components previously had encountered no such jeopardy.

Open University

Troubles multiplied for Continuing Education at San José State University. Robert J. Donovan, assistant to Continuing Education Dean Bohn, had energetically converted a struggling program, "Concurrent Enrollment," into a highly popular offering. Donovan renamed it "Open University," sold the program to the campus department chairs and reduced the paperwork to merely the teacher's signature. For enrolling a few non-matriculated students into otherwise empty seats, the academic departments earned an agreed-upon share of the standard continuing education fees. The beauty of the arrangement was that the income was generated without overhead. Professorial grousing seldom arose because the cooperating departments used the funds to support faculty teaching and research. Through Open University anyone could register and for the fee involved could take almost any course offered across the massive curriculum of the university. As early as 1973 more than 1,100 courses in 41 departments were available and the program's trajectory was up. Only impacted programs such as nursing and engineering were largely excluded.[36]

What jeopardized this arrangement was the post-Proposition 13, anti-tax pressures which popular sentiment exerted upon the state legislature. As it began redirecting the funds previously available for higher education to the revenue-starved local school districts, the California State Department of Finance trolled for additional revenue sources. Open University was too available to overlook.

TWO WAYS TO ENTER
SAN JOSE STATE UNIVERSITY
THIS SPRING

FORMAL UNIVERSITY ADMISSION

For persons seeking a University degree

- Spring 1986 semester application deadline is January 3 for all new and returning students
- Furnish test scores, official transcripts, etc., by January 10
- Admission file must be completed by January 17 to avoid a late fee
- Spring 1986 semester begins Thursday, January 23, 1986
- Get an admission application at any local high school, community college, or call the SJSU Office of Admissions (at the numbers below) or stop by the office at South Fourth Street and East San Fernando Street. Office hours are 9 a.m. - 6:45 p.m., Monday-Thursday; 9 a.m. - 5 p.m., Friday.
- New and returning students must purchase a University schedule of classes at the Spartan Bookstore in the Student Union. (The Open University schedule of classes does not list all courses).

For further information:
Office of Admissions and Records
San Jose State University
(408) 277-3268 or (408) 277-3273

OPEN UNIVERSITY ADMISSION

For persons not currently seeking a University degree

- New to the area, or just want to try University life?
- Want a chance to advance in your career, or change jobs?
- Open University offers you thousands of semester-long University courses
- Easy admission—on a space-available basis
- Weekday and weekday evening courses
- No formal University admission required
- Register at the first class session
- Any course prerequisites are noted in the catalog

For further information:
Office of Continuing Education
(408) 277-2182

For a free Open University schedule:
(408) 277-3000

Open University is a program of San Jose State University, Office of Continuing Education, a self-supporting organization.

SPRING SEMESTER BEGINS JANUARY 23

No tax money was used to produce this advertisement.

San Jose Mercury News advertisement for Open University and traditional SJSU admission, December 22, 1985.

Following preliminary skirmishes between the finance department and the state university system, the finance department placed a two million-dollar levy upon Open University. Rather than extract that amount directly from continuing education, it merely reduced the system's annual budget by a similar amount and instructed the chancellor's office to use Open University funds to make up the difference. This budget action remained permanent. The prorated cost to San José State University's Continuing Education Office became $300,000 annually. This assessment was in addition to previous taxes that had reached 10 percent of total income: four percent to the campus, four percent to the chancellor's office and two percent to the state's general fund. The percentage figures represented what the recipients concluded continuing education owed them in indirect overhead costs for items such as utilities, custodial services, office space and administrative services. Of course, the department of finance used the same rationale for the two million-dollar annual extractions. But, with or without grounds, the state needed money and was capable of taking it.[37]

As early as 1971 conversations among campus and system administrators referred to continuing education programs as the "geese that lay golden eggs."[38] As the years advanced, egg gathering became so intense that the geese considered themselves and their operations to be in mortal jeopardy. Continuing education deans could easily view the educational hierarchy as an ever-lengthening queue of money seekers. Academic vice presidents, university presidents, the chancellor and a state department of finance all had their needs and all applied the touch. Setting aside the condition of the system's revenue fund, the off-the-top percentage payments and the annual back filling to state finance, continuing education operating costs also accelerated. At this point a mini-gold rush ensued.

Competition Emerges

Television Education Network broadcast classroom on SJSU campus, 1994.

Observing Open University payments going directly to their subordinate departments, the campus academic deans chose to partake. More focused, President Gail Fullerton instructed Dean Bohn to initiate an off-campus degree program by television. The Continuing Education Revenue Fund met the start-up costs, $300,000 for then-current microwave technology. Faculty salaries for the continuing education courses rose. So, too, did rental costs for instructional space which was no longer either free or available on campus. Even more threatening, educational competitors drawn to Silicon Valley challenged the very income sources that egg gathering assumed. University of California Berkeley and Santa Cruz Extension programs remained competitive and The University of Phoenix and National University became aggressive. Rivals even advertised their courses in the *Spartan Daily*, the San José State University student newspaper.

Competition even emerged from within. In 1983 the new, focused Dean of the School of Business Marshal J. Burak unfolded an off-campus MBA program. The student-friendly graduate program resulted from extensive consultation with local business and industry leaders and was an attempt to recruit Silicon Valley engineers and business executives. The sponsor was San José State University's School of Business, not Continuing Education. The School of Engineering, under Dean Jay D. Pinson, already enjoyed networking throughout Silicon Valley and hosted off-campus degree programs.[39]

Golden Egg Syndrome

The "golden egg" syndrome had a reverse perspective as well, from the point of view of the gatherers. If Continuing Education programs had created a function of the university that was profitable, then the income should be applied elsewhere within the same university. Obtaining funding from a resource-generating arm of the same institution was hardly illegal or unethical. After all, the objective was the advancement of the recognized functions of the university. But no shared or over-riding philosophy accompanied each of the many ad hoc settlements. Each encounter of egg gatherers and egg producers created its own rules of engagement.

In her "Epilogue," California State University Continuing Education historian Salner summarized the sad state of affairs in 1988:

...the fiscal picture for continuing education in the CSU appears as mixed as policies and definitions. There is no clear agreement among educators or state policy-makers about what continuing education is, who [sic] it serves, how, why, or who should pay for it. The result is that it is very difficult to assess where continuing education currently fits in the overall picture of the 19-campus CSU system.[40]

Continuing Education at San José State University had traveled a great distance since President Dailey and the faculty boarded the "Truckee" in 1909 and set out for summer travel. In 1988, though, Dailey's successors languished at an unwelcome stopping point.

Chapter Seven

Modern Team, Modern Practices

When central organizations falter or succumb to distraction, capable subordinates exercise self-direction. This occurred within Continuing Education at San José State University. The California State University System was not dysfunctional. It only appeared so to managers disenchanted with the 1,000-Mile Consortium and California State Department of Finance paybacks.

San José State University's Continuing Education management team was capable of full cooperation with the chancellor's office in matters that advanced both the individual campus programs and the well-being of the California State University System at large. When the system seemed to be going astray that same leadership became the voice of loyal opposition.

Key Player Role

Starting in 1968 and extending to his retirement in 1992, Dean Ralph C. Bohn grew to become San José State University's key player. Through his two years as associate dean and 22 years as dean of Continuing Education, Bohn demonstrated how capacity and energy advanced programs.

Bohn's San José State University career began in 1955, teaching in the Industrial Studies Department. During his initial decade on campus he rose to full professor and chair of his department. He became very active in regional and national professional associations, acquired outside funding for sponsored programs and served on the major campus committees that selected the top administrators of the university.

Partaking in President Robert D. Clark's administrative reorganization plan in 1968, Bohn chose to be a candidate for the Continuing Education deanship. The process, though, became rather murky. By opening up all reorganized administrative positions to fresh aspirants and to former occupants, President Clark tried to avoid the unpleasantness of removing unsuitable incumbents from offices they had come to control. This strategy allowed Clark to retain Executive Vice President William J. Dusel and replace Dean of the College John W. Gilbaugh. Clark's oral history memoirs suggest that he may have designed the strategy with Dean Gilbaugh in mind. These otherwise successful procedures created some awkwardness, though, for the deanship in Continuing Education. The incumbent, History and Political Science Professor Leo P. Kibby, sought to retain the reorganized position. He had stepped into the large shoes of retiring Joe H. West and wisely followed West's management model. Kibby was reliable, traditional and personable; and he was to retire in two years.

President Clark and his new Academic Vice President Hobert W. Burns retained Kibby and they did more. Looking to the future and to the high energy Bohn, they appointed him as associate dean to Kibby. In a manner suggestive of the papacy anointing a youthful coadjutor with right of succession to a senior bishopric, Clark and Burns guided Continuing Education's transition from early modern into the program's modern blossoming. This transition took the remaining quarter of the 20th century.

Blueprint for Innovation and Expansion

Anointed or not, Bohn believed in delegation and team effort while in pursuit of innovation and expansion. He was fortunate with those he found already in the office and with his own subsequent appointees. Dean Kibby's administrative assistant, Paul M. Bradley, remained. Bradley matured on the job, with mentoring from both Kibby and Bohn. He represented Continuing Education during Bohn's leaves and other absences and upon Bohn's retirement in 1992 he served as interim dean until a fully satisfactory new dean arrived four full years later. At the start of his lengthy career Bradley learned the details of Continuing Education first hand. Later, in mid-career, he learned empathy with the clientele. As a fully employed adult himself, Bradley earned his master's degree at San José State University and his doctorate at the University of Washington.

Dr. Frank G. Willey had arrived earlier, in 1954, and focused exclusively on the management and growth of the courses offered under the specific Continuing Education rubric. Willey did not deal with Summer Session. Bohn's first management recruit was Robert J. Donovan who, with James Beck, rounded out Bohn's Continuing Education management team. This was the team that advanced the interests of Continuing Education and the community it served. Willey, the oldest and first to retire, observed in 1976 that he had organized 6,600 classes that served more than 200,000 students. This number that sparked his pride during his career-ending interview was all the more remarkable because Willey served in an era that preceded certificate programs. Beck advanced those via clustered courses. Willey's classes were mostly individual, one-time events that seldom bundled courses into certificates.[41]

Willey's insistence upon absolute control of his clearly identified administrative domain actually meshed well with Bohn's approach to management. Reminiscing from retirement, Bradley put the matter this way:

> Ralph's thing was, 'Here's what we're going to do. You guys are responsible....' It wasn't that he didn't care. It was, 'I have given you this responsibility. Let me know when it's a success.' We would create the success, and things would be fine. He wasn't a guy who wanted periodic reports....

Frank G. Willey,
Head of Extension Services

He wanted success, and he pretty much left you out there to create it, which happened. And it happened all the time.[42]

Computerizing Summer School Registration

The computerization of Summer School registration became the first major technology innovation for Continuing Education as well as a demonstration of success by the Bohn formula. The result put Continuing Education in the leadership position among its statewide colleagues and remained a campus model for the university's lingering paper and pencil approach. The interesting part, too often lost in institutional histories, was Bradley's inside account of the innovation process itself.

Dean Kibby told dean-in-waiting Bohn to find out how computers could assist their labor-intensive registrations. Bohn considered the task and assigned it to Bradley who set about discovering how to do it. In his own words, Bradley "knew zilch" about computers then.

While exploring campus assets Bradley met Doug Hartshorn, a computer programmer in Registrar John C. Montgomery's office. Hartshorn and Montgomery knew a programmer at the neighboring Bank of America, and they interested him in the project. The novelty of the challenge drew together the curious and out of this mix came Continuing Education Advanced Registration.

First, the office staff converted student registration forms into key punch cards. Then, every Tuesday night during pre-registration, Bradley and Hartshorn carried the cards to the bank. Hartshorn would man the console. Bradley would insert the cards. And out came an updated registration report. Bradley vividly recalled that, "In an hour or so we would walk back to campus with this pile of paper. It was great…actually kind'a fun. I was sort of the box carrier! And we were on the cutting edge in the system."[43]

Starting Distance Programs

Another statewide innovation, major in its results, emerged from the playful insights of Bohn and Bradley. Title V of the California State Education Code authorized what the California public colleges and universities could do. Bohn's observation, shared by the Continuing Education deans within the system, was that the need for their products had already expanded beyond the confines of Title V. Under the code restrictions, Continuing Education offered spring and fall courses for what was called continuing education credit. Only Summer School courses carried transferable academic credit. The educational needs of working adults were huge and, clearly, the statewide system's efforts via the consortium were not meeting this need. In the absence of campus initiatives that were actually suppressed by Title V, competing programs of private universities were developing the field out from under San José State University and other campuses.

Bohn's innovative spirit already pushed the limits of the legislative authorization. Through his professional associations Bohn's networking extended beyond the Continental U.S. to Puerto Rico. There, educators wanted to establish a program in professional education from which their students would emerge with a teaching credential and a master's degree. Having been consulted, Bohn discussed the matter with his management team and with appropriate campus administrators and faculty. He concluded that Continuing Education could certainly do the job. But what about Title V? The code hardly envisioned off shore start-ups.

Here Bohn's calculated risk-taking emerged. Title V authorized summer sessions and, wasn't it always summer in Puerto Rico? Following this rationalization, innovative enough in itself, Continuing Education organized and delivered the program that Puerto Rico desired. What Bohn might push for San José State University, however, was not what the Chancellor's Office Dean of Continuing Education Ralph Mills would risk for the statewide system. Mills and the deans at campuses besides San José State University were, of course, more than interested. So, they remained in discussions with Bohn over the problem. The spark of innovation came, however, from Bohn and Bradley.[44]

Starting Special Session

Mills and the deans at the other campuses were discouraged at the thought of getting the California legislature to amend the education code in their favor. Lengthy committee efforts at drafting appropriate language to liberalize Title V rendered the old language more convoluted without increasing the prospect of legislative change. According to Bradley, the deans mostly talked. The Bohn-Bradley flash took place, not at a deans' meeting, but rather in flight to one in Long Beach.

Instead of trying to redraft various sections of the state education code and then face the arduous task of prevailing upon the state assembly and senate to adopt those changes and then have the governor sign the bill, why not just keep it simple? Do not redraft Title V. Merely change one word. Change "summer" in the summer session authorization to "special," as in special session. After the time and mental energy already expended in code redrafting, such simplicity could offend the committee members and chairs. Bohn and Bradley thought that stealth would be better than bravado.

Bradley recalled that meeting vividly. After more talk and no action, Mills and the campus deans became mildly fatigued and showed signs of their frustration. Catching Bohn's smile, Bradley spoke up, observing that the problem should not be such a big deal. "All you have to do is to change the word 'Summer' to 'Special.' I was just a second banana, didn't carry any weight except I could say stuff like that." Everyone pondered and then nodded, so Mills gathered a committee that included Bohn to work on the idea. Bohn carried the winning solution through the California legislature via then-San José assemblyman and long-term friend of San José State University John Vasconcellos.[45]

The revised Title V of the state education code converted Summer Session into the expansiveness of Special Session. The significance of this change to Continuing Education and to the students it educated was extraordinary. Time, place and mode ceased being archaic limits to the education of adults in California. Special Session allowed any degree on campus to be taken off campus, anywhere and give not an extension degree, but a degree from the university. Fractions of degree programs or customized non-degree courses, likewise, became equally available.

Solving Problems for Working Adults

This solution, of course, resolved two long-standing problems: how to provide higher education to working adults and how to provide credits that adults and their employers would value. Working adults could acquire university degrees rather than merely extension credits. The academic integrity of their coursework, the same courses offered in regular sessions, rested with the academic administration of the university and its accrediting agency, the Western Association of Schools and Colleges. Internal conflict within the university over credits and course content ceased. Growth and innovation took hold immediately and would explode with the technological advances of Silicon Valley.

The Bohn-Bradley inspiration and their dexterity at advancing it created educational opportunities for working adults that the consortium failed to deliver. Under this innovation, for example, Business Dean Burak and Engineering Dean Pinson advanced their off-campus, industry-friendly graduate programs. Opportunities abounded: conferences, seminars, cruises, workshops and customized educational packages for adults in specialty fields yet to emerge from an economy discovering information technology. This small change in wording unleashed the future.

The consortium and Special Session differed in several ways. Working adults were limited in the sense that they could not skip around among the 1,000 miles of campuses. Most took classes in the evening, many in their own corporate meeting rooms. Sometimes they took classes on company time. And Special Session was not state supported. What San José State University's Continuing Education program had learned in the 1920s remained true in the 1990s. Adult students wanted something special and were willing to pay for it. Special Session gave birth to improved marketing and a successful business model.

Expanding Continuing Education Marketing

When Bohn and Bradley first became acquainted during 1968, Continuing Education had no marketing capability of its own. The president's office had one graphic artist. To develop a brochure, Continuing Education had to beg access.

When completed, the draft traveled to the state printing office in Sacramento and everyone waited. Bohn and Bradley wanted a different, more responsive system.

They first tried marketing programs with the help of interim staff. Finally they hired Diane McNutt, who had some public relations experience in the university president's office. She was to go on to create her own marketing firm, practice journalism and later enjoy elective office as the mayor of Los Gatos. Along with McNutt, Continuing Education added a full-time graphic artist.

The power of early marketing was best illustrated by the success it contributed to the languishing concurrent enrollment program, the one whose success the State Department of Finance tapped. Robert Donovan's first question when he became responsible for the program had been, "What good was a program that no one ever heard of?" Then he wondered what would happen if he brought concurrent enrollment to people's attention. "Why," he asked, "should they become interested in something with such a bad name?" By appropriating the name Open University from the long-established British university program, Donovan took care of the easy part. Next, he explored advertising and obtained campus authorization to advertise on a scale far larger than for any previous project. McNutt, managing the marketing campaign, placed advertisements with radio and television stations and the print media. Marketing then created the Open University schedule of classes that rivaled the regular San José State University schedule in size and sophistication. The total impact, name change and hustle, revitalized the program.[46]

Donovan presided over the right mix: cooperative departments, targeted students and extensive marketing. While director, he documented their impact on student enrollments, noting the program growth from a 1972 total of 149. By the 2005/2006 academic year, Open University enrollments reached 5,536,[47] making Donovan proud of the financial stability these numbers assured.

ESL Challenge

Donovan faced another challenge when he attempted to market the English as a second language program, Studies in American Language, to foreign students. Early contracts with Japanese students and young professionals established the program. An abundant pool of Middle Eastern students followed. Before e-mail and the Internet, Donovan relied heavily on marketing by mail. The program posted attractive brochures ("Learn English in California!") abroad for distribution at U.S. embassies, consulates and special prep schools. Inventively, Donovan also drafted wandering faculty. One teacher particularly, Cheryl McKenzie, who spent summers traveling with her airline pilot spouse, sprinkled the globe with enticing announcements.

And as decades and generations passed, successful foreign graduates of Studies in American Language generated more new recruits. Those who, in youth, lived and studied in California recommended San José State University to friends and relatives. The program grew from 15–20 Japanese students in 1975 to 600 SAL students representing 25 or more countries in 2006.[48]

In sum, by the 1960s, Continuing Education had become a complex unit. It had served many communities in California and abroad. It offered flexible programs that

Early Studies in American Language poster.

responded to the needs of learners. It extended the services of San José State University to traditional Continuing Education audiences such as teachers. And it stretched beyond that constituency to serve a variety of adult learners—engineers, corporate executives, government employees, small business owners—in the emerging economy of Silicon Valley.

Chapter Eight

Beyond Modernity

Historical dates, titles, functions and the participants of our story have become clarified through a blend of traditional historical methodology and information technology. At the start, even the subject matter suffered by lack of definition. Should it be called extension, continuing education, extension services, international and extended studies? When and what should be capitalized? An historical exploration from Minns' Evening Normal School to San José State University within the California State University System, conceivably, might limit itself to name changes and the conditions that prompted them. Fortunately for the institution that negotiated this maze, George Minns was then. Joe West and the Ralph Bohn team were later. And Mark Novak and his team existed at the time of publication. Throughout the story, leadership has been appropriate to the times.

New Title and Focus

Mark Novak accepted appointment as Dean of Continuing Education on August 1, 1996. His official title became Dean of Extended Studies and Associate Vice President for International Studies in 2002. At that time the name of the unit became International and Extended Studies. Summer School ended under the auspices of Continuing Education in favor of year-round university operations. Special Session expanded and diversified further. The international dimension of the university became an Extended Studies responsibility that led to growth.

The new dean's recruitment had been the most rigorous in the long history of the program. Also, it was laborious and reflected the challenges of the all-too-frequent presidential searches. The process that selected Novak, in fact, had to be repeated. Those candidates who emerged from the first national search appeared seasoned and reliable. But to the experienced insiders, all applicants lacked the energy and the leadership potential they expected. They wanted leadership that would bring their successful program up to the next level of innovation. The program insiders knew that innovation had become the survival ticket and being reliable just would not suffice.

First, the head of marketing and a major player through the Bohn-Bradley-Donovan years, Judy Rickard, a member of the search committee, appealed directly to Acting Academic Vice President James P. Walsh, who managed the search. Robert Donovan, always more overtly political, sought out President Robert L. Caret and simply told him no search finalist would do. Both had monitored the search process with great care and gave compelling arguments.[49]

President Robert L. Caret

President Caret made no appointment and Dr. Paul M. Bradley agreed to remain on as acting dean. He did so until the second search, an international process, located and advanced Dr. Novak. This time the outcome pleased the selection committee members, the university administration and the inside players alike.

The interview process displayed Continuing Education's best face to all of the applicants. The programs were functional and profitable. The key players were experienced hands – Dr. Paul M. Bradley, Sharon Cancilla, Judy Rickard, James Beck and Robert J. Donovan. So well did the program display itself that candidate Novak promptly asked Acting Dean Bradley if he were a candidate for the permanent position. If he were, Novak thought, why get serious? Bradley had actually remained longer in the dean's chair than he had expected and was advancing his own retirement plans.

The selection committee and the extension professionals wanted the best they could get. Certainly they wanted experience, but not a candidate awaiting retirement. A demonstrated capacity at advancing levels of continuing education management was required. Much more important, however, was that the successful candidate's career accomplishments remained ahead, in the future at San José State University. The basic conclusion was that Dr. Novak met the standards.

Dean Mark Novak

Booming Silicon Valley Days

Dr. Novak assumed the leadership of a unit that provided continuing education programs and university access to the booming economy of Silicon Valley. In the heyday of the valley's boom, non-degree certificate programs, in particular, grew. Corporations offered continuing education vouchers as a benefit in order to retain employees. The growth of non-degree programs led to the expansion of space at a new facility on Tisch Way in western San José, which replaced the first off-campus professional development center in downtown Campbell.

The first off-campus Professional Development Center, Campbell.

At its peak the Tisch Way facility served thousands of students in more than a dozen certificate programs. These programs rounded out San José State University's off-campus offerings that also included engineering programs delivered to corporate sites and off-campus MBA programs.

The second off-campus Professional Development Center, San José.

Establishing Distance Education

Provost and Vice President for Academic Affairs Linda Bain met with Novak during his first week on campus. She instructed him to begin the development of an online distance education program. The campus at that time had a television education network that offered a limited number of programs throughout the region. But the improvements in computer technology meant that other competing schools had started online degree and non-degree programs. Novak had developed and managed telephone and TV-based distance education programs in Canada. And Bain asked him to make this a first priority of his deanship.

Novak knew that anyone could rent technological services. And because technology changed so rapidly, it made no sense to invest precious university resources in the purchase of equipment. Instead of looking to the latest hardware as the key to new progress, Novak identified quality instructional design as the avenue to success in the emerging field of distance education. Skilled instructional designers would work with professors to transform their courses into online instruction. Novak sought out and hired the best instructional designer he could find. He hired Dr. Steve Zlotolow, who had a Ph.D. in instructional design, to spearhead this form of innovation. Zlotolow hired staff with instructional design expertise.

Zlotolow and his staff initiated program development in 1997. Online instruction grew each year after that. By 2006 more than 11,000 of San José State University's 30,000 students enrolled in courses that had some online component. In 1998 the university offered its first fully-online program, a Master of Science degree in Occupational Therapy. By 2006 this program had enrolled its eighth cohort and had graduated more than 150 students. Online instruction in 2006 is an integral part of the SJSU student experience. And with the development of wireless connectivity throughout the campus, students can realize the promise of online education. They can learn anywhere, anytime.

Revenue Growth

During Novak's first decade in office Continuing Education revenue grew from $10 million per year to more than $17 million per year. This made the SJSU unit the largest unit, by revenue, in the CSU. "It was never higher," Novak noted, "even in the booming 90s when Silicon Valley employees confronted us with company vouchers and demanded education." New programs continued to develop. Novak opened a second off-campus site on Lundy Avenue in north San José in 1998.

The third off-campus Professional Development Center, San José.

Changing Silicon Valley Needs

But the end of the dot.com bubble led to a decline in the demand for non-degree programs. Graduate degree programs at this time grew as laid off engineers decided to get advanced degrees. Also, other graduate programs, like the statewide Master of Library Science program, grew. This shift away from non-degree certificates to graduate degrees led to the rapid growth of Special Session graduate programs.

The title, International and Extended Studies, bestowed on the unit in 2002, expanded Continuing Education's franchise. San José State University exists in one of the most internationally diverse regions in the country. Students on campus speak more than 100 languages and come from all over the world. San José State University's location in Silicon Valley makes it a mecca for technology and business students from around the globe.

International Focus

Existing programs continued to allow students to experience international culture, travel and language while completing San José State University courses in San José or abroad. International Programs and Services oversees programs that allow students to study in more than 40 countries each year. Students earn SJSU resident credit while paying normal SJSU fees. They immerse themselves in another culture and learn a new language for an academic year, a semester, a summer or a short-term experience.

International House, a co-ed residence for 70 international and American students, accommodates undergraduate, graduate and English as a Second Language students from more than 35 countries each year. International House allows U.S. and international students to learn language and culture from each other while attending San José State University.

The early years of the 21st century saw a growth of international students at San José State University. By 2006 the university had more than 1,500 international (visa) students. This meant that it ranked 2nd in the United States (among similar institutions) in the number of international students. International and Extended Studies began a number of initiatives designed to further internationalize the campus.

San José State University's International House student residence.

In 2003 International and Extended Studies enrolled San José State University in the American Council on Education's "Internationalization Collaborative," which consisted of 40 institutions of higher education in the U.S., whose goals include the internationalization of campus curriculum and campus life. International and Extended Studies took the lead for SJSU in this project. Internationalization activities include the development and application of an internationalization index designed to measure San José State University's progress in internationalization. Another project was the development of a program to increase the knowledge of international communication for front-line staff. The development of a Global Studies Initiative (GSI) allowed International and Extended Studies to develop and receive approval to offer a Bachelor of Arts degree in Global Studies at San José State University.

The university also attracted adult students from mainland China, a growing world power in the early 21st century. Government and education leaders came to San José State University from China to enroll in International and Extended Studies' International Leadership Program. These officials spent four to six months on campus learning American methods of public and academic administration. Enrollment in these programs grew each year. In the first three years, the program educated 140 officials from many regions of China including Hunan, Yunnan and Shandong provinces.[50]

Any thorough description of what International and Extended Studies became by 2006 could fatigue the reader or listener. Continuing Education at San José State University grew into a vast, diverse and sophisticated set of programs that challenge any easy description.

Archived Web Site

An interested reader needs to look at the accessible archived Web site for 2006 to grasp the scope and scale of the enterprise at that time. Paraphrasing the Minns' Evening Normal School's schoolteachers starting their lessons, "Students, please open your computer to San José State University International and Extended Studies."

Its sesquicentennial Web site link is:

www.ies.sjsu.edu/history/2006

Start browsing!

You can browse the full historical record of Continuing Education at the time of this publication. And you can tailor your search of the information to your needs. This individualization is offered to the sesquicentennial explorer of the moment as well as to the dedicated scholar of the future. The researcher may discover greater depth of field from within International and Extended Studies' annual reports.

Increased Competition

Continuing Education became a high-stakes enterprise. Novak and his management team guided the program through a soft landing at the conclusion of the 1990s dot.com mania. Risks have been real in the continuing education business. In Continuing Education's post-modern age, they became greater.

Still, even after the dot.com bust, careful management of SJSU's Continuing Education unit led to fiscal growth. International and Extended Studies showed a gross income of $17 million in 2005. This revenue and the financial successes of past years led to a fiscal reserve fund of $12 million in 2005. The modern high stakes game required high quality management with an ever-increasing level of academic, personnel, finance, marketing and diplomatic competence.

At San José State University, academic and community programs remained vital, but this no longer sufficed. Past leaders had created and bequeathed an expanding and academically sound program. Novak appreciated all that was bequeathed, but he also looked to further innovation.

At the start of the continuing education enterprise in 1857, George Minns told schoolteachers each Monday night what they had to teach for the week ahead. At the sesquicentennial, Dean Novak, through his management team, asked the students what they wanted to learn for their lifetime ahead. What they chose is no longer available on Monday nights at the evening normal school - it is available all the time, everywhere.[51]

Afterword

The values of access, international programs and innovation continue to guide Continuing Education, now International and Extended Studies, at San José State University. Educational needs continue to evolve. Changes in society, technology and life expectancy all demand educational innovation. The core university programs ensure stability. Mechanisms exist to ensure that the curriculum remains relatively the same from year to year—even generation to generation. Continuing Education, through International and Extended Studies, serves a unique function on the campus today. It allows the campus to experiment with change, to create programs that meet the needs of unique clients (like business and industry), to develop interdisciplinary degrees, to offer programs that use new technologies and to encourage the use of experimental teaching methods. Continuing Education makes all of this possible with little bureaucratic fuss.

Continuing Education also supports programs that the university's general fund cannot support. A new biotechnology master's degree, for example, relied on self-support revenue to start up and survive in its early years. The high cost of the program, the small number of students in the program and the high cost of laboratory instruction meant that state-approved fees could not cover the program's costs. Continuing Education's Special Session category allowed for higher fees that made this program possible.

The online occupational therapy master's degree program offers another example of innovation—this time technological. This program represents the first online master's degree offered by San José State University (fully approved by the Western Association of Schools and Colleges). The program graduated its seventh cohort in 2006. More than 100 students have graduated from this program since it first began in 1998. Students from all over the world and from many states throughout the United States have completed this master's degree.

Many programs that began long ago—Open University, Studies in American Language, the off-campus MBA and the master's degree in engineering to name a few examples—continue today. Past deans and administrators succeeded in institutionalizing these programs so that they became a part of San José State University's academic fabric. Still, each year new programs emerge. Some of these will gain institutional status and form part of the regular curriculum. A new global studies bachelor's degree program quickly attracted more than 30 students who selected it as their major field. Its future looks promising. Other programs will serve a need for some time and then fade away.

Two of our newest programs extend the range of International and Extended Studies' mission by reaching out to new groups—in this case pre-college young people and older adult learners, those at both ends of the career spectrum.

Continuing Education at San José State University will continue to evolve. It will seek out community needs and respond to requests for higher education. It will stretch the reach of San José State University into new communities within and beyond the United States. No one can predict the future direction of continuing education because no one can predict the courses, programs or topics that people will need and want in the future. But the core values of access, international programs and innovation will undoubtedly guide future developments.

As one link in the chain of Continuing Education leadership, my staff and I will serve the present and prepare for the future. Dr. Walsh's history will guide future leaders of Continuing Education at San José State University by showing them their tradition and their place in the university. This history also shows that the core values of Continuing Education and San José State University, as Dr. Walsh so aptly says, are "one and the same."

Mark Novak

Dean and Associate Vice President
International and Extended Studies
San José State University
San José, California
2006

The Timeline of Continuing Education Leadership 1857–2006

1857–1862
George W. Minns, San Francisco educator, directs California's first public institution of higher education, Minns' Evening Normal School, as a continuing education function.

1863–1902
Years during which only regular Normal School classes were offered.

1903–1919
Morris E. Dailey, president, San José State University, founds and directs the first California State Normal School Summer Session, 1903. Dailey organizes and leads European travel study, 1909.

1920–1925
Leadership remains in the campus president's office during four brief administrations: **William W. Kemp** (1920-1923), **Alexander R. Heron** (summer 1923), **Edwin R. Snyder** (1923-1925), **Herman F. Minssen** (1925). Minssen provides continuity as a mathematics professor, college business secretary, financial director of Summer School and then assistant to the president, vice president and acting president through 1927.

1925–1936
George E. Freeland, professor of education, teaches and assumes management responsibilities in Summer School and in modern Continuing Education.

1936–1941
Depression Era programs revert to the campus president's office under **Thomas W. MacQuarrie**. **William H. Poytress**, professor of economics, is the program's face to the community.

1942–1947
Joe H. West, while college registrar, manages Summer School and Continuing Education.

1948–1953

Raymond M. Mosher, professor of psychology, becomes the first full-time director of Summer School. Mosher's title becomes dean of Educational Services and Summer Sessions with the college administrative reorganization of 1950.

1953–1954

William G. Sweeney, professor of education, serves as acting dean of Educational Services and Summer Sessions.

1954–1965

Joe H. West, professional administrator, assumes exclusively the direction of Educational Services and Summer Sessions. Dean West manages an expanded office: Summer School, Continuing Education, the college library and audiovisual services.

1965–1970

Leo P. Kibby, scholar and administrator, becomes acting dean of Educational Services and Summer Sessions. Dean Kibby accepts permanent appointment within the college administrative reorganization of 1968 and **Ralph C. Bohn** becomes associate dean.

1970–1992

Ralph C. Bohn, a department chairman and program developer, serves as the first dean of Continuing Education to invest a career in the management and expansion of the office and its programs.

1992–1996

Paul M. Bradley, a career professional in continuing education, advances technology and innovation as acting dean during the dot.com boom.

1996–2006

Mark Novak, administrator and scholar, becomes the seventh full-time dean of Continuing Education. Dean Novak's title is changed to Dean of Extended Studies and Associate Vice President for International Studies in 2002. The office is renamed International and Extended Studies. Summer Session ceases being a function of Continuing Education. Entrepreneurialism expands.

From Minns' Evening Normal School to San José State University

1857
George W. Minns heads California's first public institution of higher education, Minns' Evening Normal School, located in San Francisco.

1862
Minns' Evening Normal School becomes the California State Normal School.

1871
The California State Normal School moves to San José.

1881
A branch campus of the California State Normal School is established in Los Angeles. This branch later becomes University of California, Los Angeles.

1887
The California State Normal School becomes San José State Normal School.

1921
San José State Normal School is renamed San José State Teachers College.

1935
San José State Teachers College becomes San José State College.

1961
San José State College is incorporated into the California State Colleges system.

1972
San José State College becomes California State University, San José, achieving university status.

1974
California State University, San José is renamed San José State University.

Footnotes

Chapter One: One and the Same

1 - *Alta California*, August 13, 1853, as quoted by Helen Bullock Waldie, "Education in San Francisco, 1850-1860: A Study of Frontier Attitudes," M. A. thesis, Stanford, 1953, p. 95.

2 - *Annual Report of the Superintendent of Public Schools to the Board of Education* (San Francisco: 1854), p. 20; (1858), pp.19–22.

3 - HYPERLINK "http://www.cable-car-guy.com/html/ccwho.html#hxc" http://www.cable-car-guy.com/html/ccwho.html#hxc

4 - HYPERLINK "http://www.noehill.com/sf/landmarks/sf051.asp" http://www.noehill.com/sf/landmarks/sf051.asp

5 - HYPERLINK http://freepages.genealogy.rootsweb.com/~npmelton/marr72d.htm http://freepages.genealogy.rootsweb.com/~npmelton/marr72d.htm

6 - HYPERLINK "http://rochlin-roots-west.com/gallery/index.shtml" http://rochlin-roots-west.com/gallery/index.shtml

Chapter Two: Watching and Waiting

7 - Kathleen Rockhill, *Academic Excellence and Public Service: A History of University Extension in California* (New Brunswick and London: Transaction Books, 1983), p. 27.

8 - *San Jose Daily Mercury*, Dec. 8, 1892, p. 6; Apr.19, 1894, p. 6.

9 - HYPERLINK "http://www2.asanet.org/governance/ross.htm" http://www2.asanet.org/governance/ross.htm

Chapter Three: The Critical Choice

10 - Benjamin F. Gilbert, *Pioneers for One Hundred Years: San José State College, 1857–1957* (San José: San José State College, 1957), p. 23.

11 - "First Recommendation for a Summer Session, A Report of President James McNaughton, March 22, 1900," Benjamin F. Gilbert, Centennial Notes, Special Collections, Dr. Martin Luther King, Jr. Library, San José, California.

12 - Gilbert, *Pioneers for One Hundred Years: San José State College, 1857–1957*, p.106.

13 - "Dailey's Recommendation for a Summer Session, A Report of Morris Elmer Dailey, March 21, 1901," Benjamin F. Gilbert, Centennial Notes, Special Collections, Dr. Martin Luther King, Jr. Library, San José, California.

14 - Gilbert, *Pioneers for One Hundred Years: San José State College, 1857–1957*, p.113.

15 - Gilbert notes from *San Jose Daily Mercury*, June 30, 1903; "Dailey's Recommendations for a Summer Session, A Report of Morris Elmer Dailey, March 21, 1901," Benjamin F. Gilbert, Centennial Notes, Special Collections, Dr. Martin Luther King, Jr. Library, San José, California.

16 - Gilbert notes from *San Jose Herald*, July 9, 1903, Special Collections, Dr. Martin Luther King, Jr. Library, San José, California.

17 - *Mercury Herald*, July 23, 1943, in "Summer School Scrap Book," p. 44, Special Collections, Dr. Martin Luther King, Jr. Library, San José, California.

18 - *Mercury Herald*, June 26, 1934, p. 43; July 26,1934, p. 47; July 29, 1934, pp. 47–48; July 29, 1935, p. 63, in "Summer School Scrap Book;" Thomas W. MacQuarrie, "Memo to Faculty," August 2, 1937, in "Summer School Scrap Book," p.103, Special Collections, Dr. Martin Luther King, Jr. Library, San José, California.

19 - Marcia Salner, *Continuing Education in the California State University: A History*, (Long Beach: California State University, 1988), p. 53.

20 - *San Jose Mercury*, March 21, 1954, in Herman F. Minssen, "University Scrap Book," p. 97, Special Collections, Dr. Martin Luther King, Jr. Library, San José, California.

21 - *San Jose Mercury*, June 11, 1965, in Minssen, "University Scrap Book," p. 103, Special Collections, Dr. Martin Luther King, Jr. Library, San José, California.

22 - *San Jose Mercury*, May 31, 1970, Minssen, "University Scrap Book," p. 3, Special Collections, Dr. Martin Luther King, Jr. Library, San José, California.

23 - *Mercury Herald*, July 13, 1932, in "Summer School Scrap Book," p. 19, Special Collections, Dr. Martin Luther King, Jr. Library, San José, California.

24 - *Mercury Herald*, June 27, 1933, in "Summer School Scrap Book," p. 30, Special Collections, Dr. Martin Luther King, Jr. Library, San José, California; Salner, *Continuing Education*, p. 16.

25 - *Mercury Herald*, October 9, 1942, Minssen, "University Scrap Book," p. 9, Special Collections, Dr. Martin Luther King, Jr. Library, San José, California.

26 - *Mercury Herald*, May 23, 1942, Minssen, "University Scrap Book," p. 55, Special Collections, Dr. Martin Luther King, Jr. Library, San José, California.

27 - *Mercury Herald*, August 7, 1946, Minssen, "University Scrap Book," p. 88, and August 10, 1946, p. 90, Special Collections, Dr. Martin Luther King, Jr. Library, San José, California.

Chapter Four: What Came First?

28 - *San Jose Daily Mercury*, June 15, 1909, p. 5.

29 - *San Jose Mercury and Herald*, June 27, 1909, p. 5; *San Jose Daily Mercury*, June 15, 1909, p. 5.

30 - *San Jose Daily Mercury*, September 1, 1909, p. 4.

31 - *Mercury*, September [n.d.], 1925, in Minssen, "University Scrap Book," p. 45, Special Collections, Dr. Martin Luther King, Jr. Library, San José, California; James C. DeVoss, Personnel Action File, Office of Faculty Affairs, San José State University.

32 - G.A. "Bill" McCallum, "Field Studies in Natural History (West Coast School of Nature Study)," ms p. 16, Biology Department, San José State University.

Chapter Six: Price of Success

33 - Salner, *Continuing Education in the California State University: A History*, pp. 135–139.

34 - Salner, *Continuing Education in the California State University: A History*, pp. 46–49.

35 - Salner, *Continuing Education in the California State University: A History*, p. 125.

36 - *San Jose Mercury*, February 2, 1973 and *San Jose Mercury*, September 8, 1976, Minnsen, "University Scrap Book," p. 11 and p. 185, Special Collections, Dr. Martin Luther King, Jr. Library, San José, California; Interview, Robert J. Donovan, May 11, 2005, Aptos, California.

37 - *Summer Times*, July 9, 1986, pp. 3 and 8, Special Collections, Dr. Martin Luther King, Jr. Library, San José, California.

38 - Salner, *Continuing Education in the California State University: A History*, p. 73.

39 - *San Jose Mercury*, February 7, 1983, and June 14, 1982, in Minssen, "University Scrap Book," pp. 18 and 136, Special Collections, Dr. Martin Luther King, Jr. Library, San José, California.

40 - Salner, *Continuing Education in the California State University: A History*, p. 135.

Chapter Seven: Modern Team, Modern Practices

41 - *San Jose Mercury*, December 2, 1976, in Minssen, "University Scrap Book," p. 49, Special Collections, Dr. Martin Luther King, Jr. Library, San José, California.

42 - Interview, Paul M. Bradley, April 7, 2005, San José, California.

43 - Interview, Paul M. Bradley, April 7, 2005, San José, California.

44 - Interview, Paul M. Bradley, April 7, 2005, San José, California.

45 - Interview, Paul M. Bradley, April 7, 2005, San José, California.

46 - Interview, Robert J. Donovan, May 5, 2005, Aptos, California.

47 - Robert J. Donovan, "Open University (Concurrent Enrollment) Program: Brief Background," ms in possession of author.

48 - Interview, Robert J. Donovan, May 5, 2005, Aptos, California; Figures provided by Cathy Murillo, SAL Director, May 10, 2006, San José, California; Figures provided by Karen O'Neill, SAL Associate Director, May 10, 2006, San José, California.

Chapter Eight: Beyond Modernity

49 - Interview, Judith M. Rickard, June 9, 2005, San José, California; Interview, Robert J. Donovan, May 5, 2005, Aptos, California.

50 - Interview, Mark A. Novak, June 17, 2005, San José, California.

51 - For more information see: www.ies.sjsu.edu/history/2006

Photo Credits

Chapter 1 – One and the Same

1. **George W. Minns**, San José State University Special Collections and Archives, San José, California.

2. *Eighth Annual Report of the Superintendent of Public Schools, 1858, City and County of San Francisco*, **published by the Board of Education, 1858**, San Francisco History Center, San Francisco Public Library, San Francisco, California.

3. *Eleventh Annual Report of the Superintendent of Public Schools, 1861–1862, City and County of San Francisco*, **published by the Board of Education, 1863**, San Francisco History Center, San Francisco Public Library, San Francisco, California.

4. **Minns' Evening Normal School graduates, 1861 and 1862, published in** *Eleventh Annual Report of the Superintendent of Public Schools, 1861-1862, City and County of San Francisco*, **published by the Board of Education, 1863**, San Francisco History Center, San Francisco Public Library, San Francisco, California.

5. **The first graduating class of the first high school in San Francisco, 1859**, San Francisco History Center, San Francisco Public Library, San Francisco, California.

6. **1857 Kennedy family portrait**, courtesy of Elizabeth Burke Merriman.

7. **Hannah Marks**, courtesy of the Adele and Meyer E. Solomons collection, Western Jewish History Center, Berkeley, California.

Chapter Two – Watching and Waiting

1. **First San José Normal School building, destroyed by fire in 1880**, San José State University Special Collections and Archives, San José, California.

2. **Second San José Normal School building, circa 1900**, photo by J. E. Addicott, San José State University Special Collections and Archives, San José, California.

3. **State Normal School faculty, students and visitors in Normal Hall, c. 1891**, San José State University Special Collections and Archives, San José, California.

4. **The University Extension Club of San José syllabi, 1892–1902**, San José State University Special Collections and Archives, San José, California.

5. **David Starr Jordan's University Extension Club of San José syllabus**, San José State University Special Collections and Archives, San José, California.

Chapter Three – The Critical Choice

1. **San José State Normal School Class of 1878 with State Normal School building at bottom row, center**, courtesy, History San José.

2. **San José State Normal School President Morris E. Dailey planting a tree, with Professor Henry Meade Bland at his left, wearing a skull cap**, San José State University Special Collections and Archives, San José, California.

3. **San José State Normal School President Morris E. Dailey**, San José State University Special Collections and Archives, San José, California.

4. **San José State Normal School volunteers preparing food during the influenza epidemic, 1918**, courtesy, History San José.

5. **San José State Normal School Summer School 1936 schedule of classes**, San José State University Special Collections and Archives, San José, California.

6. **San José State Normal School Summer School 1936 schedule of classes illustrative internal page**, San José State University Special Collections and Archives, San José, California.

Chapter Four – What Came First?

1. **San José State Normal School faculty and President Morris E. Dailey ready for departure on the first travel study program, June 26, 1909**, Dr. Martin Luther King, Jr., Library, California Room, San José, California.

2. **Title page, *The Story of an Inspired Past*,** by Mrs. Estelle Greathead, 1928, San José State University Special Collections and Archives, San José, California.

3. **Estelle Greathead**, San José State University Special Collections and Archives, San José, California.

4. **West Coast School of Nature Study 1936 schedule of classes**, courtesy of Field Studies in Natural History, San José State University, San José, California.

5. **G. A. "Bill" McCallum**, San José State University Special Collections and Archives, San José, California.

6. **Dwight Bentel**, San José State University Special Collections and Archives, San José, California.

7. **Science Building, San José State University, circa 1940**, San José State University Special Collections and Archives, San José, California.

8. **Joe H. West**, San José State University Special Collections and Archives, San Jose, California.

9. **M. Edd Burton**, courtesy of M. Edd Burton.

10. **Field Studies in Natural History participants, Death Valley**, courtesy of M. Edd Burton.

Chapter Five – Leadership Lineage

1. **George W. Minns**, San José State University Special Collections and Archives, San José, California.

2. **Morris E. Dailey**, San José State University Special Collections and Archives, San José, California.

3. **William W. Kemp**, San José State University Special Collections and Archives, San José, California.

4. **Alexander R. Heron**, San José State University Special Collections and Archives, San José, California.

5. **Edwin R. Snyder**, San José State University Special Collections and Archives, San José, California.

6. **Herman F. Minssen**, San José State University Special Collections and Archives, San José, California.

7. **George E. Freeland**, San José State University Special Collections and Archives, San José, California.

8. **Thomas W. MacQuarrie**, San José State University Special Collections and Archives, San José, California.

9. **William H. Poytress**, San José State University Special Collections and Archives, San José, California.

10. **Joe H. West**, San José State University Special Collections and Archives, San José, California.

11. **Raymond M. Mosher**, San José State University Special Collections and Archives, San José, California.

12. **William G. Sweeney**, San José State University Special Collections and Archives, San José, California.

13. **Leo P. Kibby**, San José State University Special Collections and Archives, San José, California.

14. **Ralph C. Bohn**, San José State University Special Collections and Archives, San José, California.

15. **Paul M. Bradley**, courtesy of Paul M. Bradley.

16. **Mark Novak**, photo by Robert Bain, San José State University Photographer.

17. **Paul Bradley, left, Mark Novak, center and Ralph Bohn, right**, photo by Sharon Hall, Sharon Hall Photography.

Chapter Six – Price of Success

1. **Continuing Education advertisement for Open University and traditional San José State University admission,** *San Jose Mercury News*, **December 22, 1985**, San José State University Special Collections and Archives, San José, California.

2. **Television Education Network broadcast classroom on San José State University campus, 1994**, courtesy of Betty Benson.

Chapter Seven – Modern Team, Modern Practices

1. **Frank G. Willey**, San José State University Special Collections and Archives, San José, California.

2. **Studies in American Language brochure**, San José State University Special Collections and Archives, San José, California.

Chapter Eight – Beyond Modernity

1. **Robert L. Caret**, photo by Sharon Hall, Sharon Hall Photography.

2. **Mark Novak**, photo by Robert Bain, San José State University Photographer.

3. **First off-campus SJSU Professional Development Center, Campbell and Winchester Avenues, Campbell**, photo by Carl Miescke.

4. **Second off-campus SJSU Professional Development Center, Tisch Way, San José**, photo by Sharon Hall, Sharon Hall Photography.

5. **Third off-campus SJSU Professional Development Center, Lundy Avenue, San José**, photo by Sharon Hall, Sharon Hall Photography.

6. **San José State University's International House student residence**, photo courtesy of International House.

Index